AQA Anthology of Poetry

Love and Relationships

As everyone knows, analysing relationships is brilliant fun.
But analysing poems about relationships? That can be daunting.

Not to worry. This brilliant book guides you through the entire cluster — form,
structure, language, themes, context... the lot. And because it's from CGP,
we get straight to the point, with no needless rambling.

We've also included plenty of practice questions to test you on what you've learned,
plus a whole section of advice to help you score a top grade in the exam.
It's the perfect partner to your poetry studies, so don't leave it on the shelf...

The Poetry Guide

CONTENTS

How To Use This Book 1

Section One — The Poems

When We Two Parted — Lord Byron 2
Love's Philosophy — Percy Bysshe Shelley 4
Porphyria's Lover — Robert Browning 6
Sonnet 29 — 'I think of thee!' — Elizabeth Barrett Browning 8
Neutral Tones — Thomas Hardy 10
The Farmer's Bride — Charlotte Mew 12
Walking Away — C. Day Lewis 14
Letters From Yorkshire — Maura Dooley 16
Eden Rock — Charles Causley 18
Follower — Seamus Heaney 20
Mother, Any Distance — Simon Armitage 22
Before You Were Mine — Carol Ann Duffy 24
Winter Swans — Owen Sheers 26
Singh Song! — Daljit Nagra 28
Climbing My Grandfather — Andrew Waterhouse 30
Practice Questions 32

Section Two — Themes

Romantic Love 36
Family Relationships 38
Distance 40
Desire and Longing 41
Getting Older 42
Death 43
Memory 44
Nature 45
Practice Questions 46

Section Three — Poetic Techniques

Forms of Poetry 49
Poetic Devices 50
Use of Sound 52
Imagery 53
Rhyme and Rhythm 54
Voice 55
Beginnings of Poems 56
Endings of Poems 57
Mood 58
Practice Questions 59

CONTENTS

Section Four — Exam Advice

The Poetry Exam 62
How to Structure Your Answer...63
How to Answer the Question 64
Planning Your Answer 67
Sample Answer 68

Section Five — Improving and Marking Sample Answers

Adding Quotes and Developing Points................................. 70
Mark Scheme... 72
Marking Answer Extracts 73
Marking a Whole Answer.. 75

Glossary.. 77
Index 79
Answers 80

Published by CGP

Editors:
Claire Boulter
Alex Fairer
Matt Topping

With thanks to Emma Bonney and Nicola Woodfin for the proofreading.
With thanks to Laura Jakubowski for the copyright research.

Acknowledgements:

Cover quote from 'When We Two Parted' by Lord Byron.

'The Farmer's Bride' by Charlotte Mew from *Charlotte Mew: Collected Poems and Selected Prose* published by Carcanet Press (1997).

'Walking Away' from *The Complete Poems* by Cecil Day-Lewis. Published by Sinclair Stevenson.
Reprinted by permission of The Random House Group Limited.

'Letters From Yorkshire' by Maura Dooley from *Sound Barrier: Poems 1982-2002* published by Bloodaxe Books, 2002.
Reproduced with permission of Bloodaxe Books on behalf of the author.

'Eden Rock' by Charles Causley from *Collected Poems* published by Macmillan, reproduced with permission from David Higham Associates Limited.

'Follower' by Seamus Heaney from *Death of a Naturalist*. Reprinted by permission of the publishers Faber and Faber Ltd.

'Mother, Any Distance' by Simon Armitage from *Selected Poems* (2001). Reprinted by permission of the publishers Faber and Faber Ltd.

'Before You Were Mine' from *Mean Time* by Carol Ann Duffy Copyright © Carol Ann Duffy 1993. Published by Picador 2013.
Reproduced by permission of the author c/o Rogers, Coleridge & White Ltd., 20 Powis Mews, London W11 1JN

'Winter Swans' from *Skirrid Hill* by Owen Sheers. Copyright © Owen Sheers 2005. Published by Seren, 2005.
Reproduced by permission of the author c/o Rogers, Coleridge & White Ltd., 20 Powis Mews, London W11 1JN

'Singh Song!' by Daljit Nagra from *Look We Have Coming to Dover!* Reprinted by permission of the publishers Faber and Faber Ltd.

'Climbing My Grandfather' by Andrew Waterhouse, from *In* (The Rialto, 2000), reproduced by permission of the Estate of Andrew Waterhouse.

AQA material is reproduced by permission of AQA.

Every effort has been made to locate copyright holders and obtain permission to reproduce sources. For those sources where it has been difficult to trace the copyright holder of the work, we would be grateful for information. If any copyright holder would like us to make an amendment to the acknowledgements, please notify us and we will gladly update the book at the next reprint. Thank you.

ISBN: 978 1 78294 362 4
Printed by Elanders Ltd, Newcastle upon Tyne.
Clipart from Corel®

Based on the classic CGP style created by Richard Parsons.

Text, design, layout and original illustrations © Coordination Group Publications Ltd. (CGP) 2015
All rights reserved.

Photocopying more than one chapter of this book is not permitted. Extra copies are available from CGP.
0800 1712 712 • www.cgpbooks.co.uk

How To Use This Book

This book is for anyone studying the 'Love and Relationships' cluster of the AQA GCSE English Literature Poetry Anthology. You'll have to answer an exam question on the poems — this book tells you what you need to know.

You need to know the poems really well

You need to know all fifteen poems <u>in depth</u>. Read each one carefully <u>over and over again</u>, and jot down your <u>own ideas</u> about it. This book will help you <u>understand</u> the poems and develop your ideas:

You can't take the poems or any notes into the exam, so you need to learn plenty of short quotes to use.

- <u>Section One</u> guides you through each poem in the cluster — read the <u>notes</u> on what each poem <u>means</u>, its main <u>features</u>, and the <u>attitudes</u> and <u>feelings</u> it conveys.
- Answer the <u>questions</u> about each poem — these will help you develop a <u>personal response</u> to it.
- When you feel that you know the poems <u>well</u>, have a go at the <u>questions</u> at the end of the section. They'll help you identify any <u>gaps</u> in your knowledge of the poems.

In the exam, you'll have to compare poems with a similar theme

1) The Poetry Anthology question will give you <u>one</u> poem from the 'Love and Relationships' cluster, and ask you to <u>choose another</u> with a <u>similar theme</u> to compare it to.

2) In <u>Section Two</u> the poems are grouped by <u>theme</u>, to give you some ideas of which poems you could <u>compare</u> in the exam and what you might say about them.

3) Have a go at the <u>practice questions</u> at the end of the section to check you're up to speed with the themes of each poem.

Have a look inside the front cover for a handy summary of which themes relate to which poems.

Get to grips with the main features of each poem

1) <u>Section Three</u> is all about <u>form</u>, <u>structure</u> and <u>language</u>.

2) It looks at how different poets use techniques like <u>rhyme</u>, <u>rhythm</u> and <u>imagery</u> to create <u>effects</u> — the examiners are <u>really keen</u> for you to write about this.

3) There are some more <u>practice questions</u> at the end of the section to help you test your knowledge.

First day on the job, and Tim had already got to grips with the 'self-destruct' feature of his car.

Learn how to write a cracking exam answer

1) You need to know <u>how</u> to write a great essay <u>comparing</u> two poems:

- <u>Section Four</u> gives you loads of <u>advice</u> on how to <u>plan</u> and <u>write</u> a fantastic exam answer.
- There are plenty of extracts from <u>sample answers</u> to show you the right way to approach the question.

2) Once you know the <u>theory</u>, put it into <u>practice</u>:

- <u>Section Five</u> lets you test your skills by <u>adding quotes</u> or <u>extending points</u> to improve essay extracts. This will help you understand how to really <u>use the poems</u> to write a <u>top-notch</u> answer.
- It also gives you some sample answers to <u>grade</u>, to help you work out how to improve your <u>own answers</u>.

3) There's no substitute for getting some practice at <u>writing essays</u>:

- Use everything you've learnt to answer the <u>exam-style questions</u> at the end of Sections One, Two and Three.
- You don't have to write a <u>full essay</u> for every question — making a <u>detailed plan</u> is still good practice.

When We Two Parted

He addresses his former lover directly, which makes the poem feel more personal. This contrasts with use of "They" in stanza 3 — this hints at a bond between the narrator and his lover which keeps them separate from others.

This could suggest that they weren't properly in love with each other. However, it's clear that the narrator was deeply affected by their parting, so perhaps he's accusing his lover of only being half in love with him. He could also be referring to himself as "Half" of the couple, meaning that he's broken-hearted and his former lover isn't.

This could mean that they had nothing to say to each other any more, but it also hints that their relationship was secret.

This violent imagery suggests that the parting was painful and traumatic for the narrator.

The narrator describes his lover like a corpse. This suggests that her feelings for him have died.

Repetition of harsh 'k' sound emphasises coldness.

Enjambment emphasises the link between past and present — this shows how his sorrow is ongoing.

The cold dew on the narrator's forehead reflects the coldness between him and his lover.

The poem switches to talk about the present.

Her reputation is damaged ("light" suggests weak and flimsy) because people know about her affairs.

Links to broken hearts in stanza 1.

He feels he's involved in her "shame" because he also had an affair with her.

Alliteration of 'sh' sound links to silence.

He hears people talking about the affairs his former lover is having — this is painful for him.

Rhetorical question emphasises how deeply he felt for her — he can't bear to hear that she's having affairs with other men.

Metaphor suggests that her name sounds like a death knell to him — it reminds him of the death of their relationship.

The narrator repeatedly addresses his former lover directly, creating the impression that he's still preoccupied by her — this shows how her actions continue to upset him.

Repetition emphasises how long he'll feel regret.

He doesn't just feel sadness — he also regrets their relationship.

Because no-one knew they were lovers, he can't talk about his pain.

He's silent because he's incapable of expressing his pain — not just because of the need for secrecy.

The poem switches to thinking about the future.

He mourns their relationship like a death.

Accusatory language suggests that he is angry with her.

Repetition from stanza 1 emphasises secrecy and sorrow — he's still hurting and is unable to move on.

When we two parted
In silence and tears,
Half broken-hearted,
To sever for years,
5 Pale grew thy cheek and cold,
Colder thy kiss;
Truly that hour foretold
Sorrow to this.

The dew of the morning
10 Sunk chill on my brow –
It felt like the warning
Of what I feel now.
Thy vows are all broken,
And light is thy fame;
15 I hear thy name spoken
And share in its shame.   Sibilance

They name thee before me,
A knell to mine ear;
A shudder comes o'er me –
20 Why wert thou so dear?
They know not I knew thee,
Who knew thee too well:
Long, long shall I rue thee,
Too deeply to tell.

25 In secret we met –
In silence I grieve,
That thy heart could forget,
Thy spirit deceive.
If I should meet thee
30 After long years,
How should I greet thee?
With silence and tears.

POEM DICTIONARY
sever — separate
foretold — predicted or foreshadowed
fame — reputation
knell — the sound of a bell rung slowly to mark a death
rue — to feel regret or sorrow over something

Lord Byron

Byron (1788-1824) published this poem in 1816, but he claimed to have written it in 1808 to conceal the identity of the woman in the poem, who was married — Byron was notorious for his scandalous affairs...

You've got to know what the poem's about

1) The narrator recalls the day he and his lover parted — she didn't seem to have any affection for him anymore. He believes the sadness that he felt then foreshadowed the sadness he feels in the present.

2) Although time has passed, even hearing her name affects the narrator deeply. He hears people talking about her affairs with other men, and he feels hurt by her actions.

3) He thinks that he'll always feel hurt — if he meets her again he'll act just the same as when they parted.

4) Byron may have been writing about Lady Frances Webster — it's rumoured they had a relationship while she was married to a friend of Byron's. She apparently went on to have an affair with the Duke of Wellington.

Learn about the form, structure and language

1) **FORM** — The poem consists of four 8-line stanzas, and has a strong ABAB rhyme scheme and regular rhythm. The rhythm emphasises certain syllables (e.g. "Cold" and "kiss" in line 6), which highlights the speaker's pain.

2) **STRUCTURE** — The poem moves through time — the narrator constantly shifts between past, present and future. The juxtaposition of the past and present emphasises that there's no change in his feelings.

3) **LANGUAGE ABOUT DEATH** — To the narrator, the end of the relationship is like death — this emphasises his former lover's lack of feeling for him. Now, even hearing her name reminds him of a death "knell".

4) **LANGUAGE OF THE SENSES** — Typical love poetry uses descriptions that are pleasing to the senses, but in this poem, the narrator uses negative descriptions, such as the sight of his lover's "pale" cheek, the cold touch of "dew" and the funereal sound of a "knell". This emphasises how he's lost love and is hurt by it.

5) **LANGUAGE ABOUT SILENCE AND SECRECY** — Silence is used to reflect how the relationship was secret — the narrator and his lover are silent when they part and the narrator is silent about their affair both in the past and in the present. This silence contrasts with the voices of his friends in the third stanza, which draws attention to the fact that the speaker is unable to express how he feels — he must stay silent about the affair.

Remember the feelings and attitudes in the poem

1) **GRIEF** — The narrator mourns the end of the relationship as though it's a death.

2) **ANGER** — The narrator seems angry that his lover has broken promises and is having affairs with other men. He imagines greeting her with silence and tears, suggesting he wants her to see how much she's hurt him.

3) **REGRET** — He regrets their relationship because of the way things turned out — he suffered a lot.

Go a step further and give a personal response

Have a go at answering these questions to help you come up with your own ideas about the poem:

Q1. Which syllables are stressed in the second stanza? What is the effect of this?
Q2. Why do you think the poet used language to do with the cold in this poem?
Q3. What impression do you get of the speaker's former lover? Do you think this is likely to be fair?

Loss, memory, death...

The narrator in 'Neutral Tones' is also affected by a painful memory of losing his lover, and expresses this loss in terms of death. In contrast, the narrator of 'Walking Away' comes to terms with a painful memory.

Love's Philosophy

Philosophy, which literally means 'love of wisdom', is a way of thinking which aims to make sense of reality and the meaning of life. In this poem, the narrator is trying to come to an understanding about love.

The narrator uses personification to draw parallels between what happens in nature and his own desire to be with his lover.

Increasing scale of imagery — showing water joining larger and larger bodies hints that loving someone makes you part of something bigger than yourself.

Imagery of flowing water shows that everything is connected to everything else.

"river" and "ever" are half-rhymes, as are "heaven" and "forgiven" in the second stanza — this reflects how the couple aren't united.

Personification suggests that nature enjoys and benefits from this union.

This line sums up the narrator's argument.

The narrator thinks it's God's law that everything in nature mingles together.

In both stanzas, the first 6 or 7 lines are confident assertions, which contrast with the rhetorical questions in the final lines.

Hints that the woman the narrator is addressing has rejected him.

Repetition highlights just how many examples he can show her of unity in nature.

Emphasises that everything is connected, even the Sun and Moon — not just nature on Earth.

The fountains mingle with the river
And the rivers with the ocean,
The winds of heaven mix for ever
With a sweet emotion;
5   Nothing in the world is single,
All things by a law divine
In one another's being mingle –
Why not I with thine?

See the mountains kiss high heaven
10   And the waves clasp one another;
No sister-flower would be forgiven
If it disdain'd its brother;
And the sunlight clasps the earth,
And the moonbeams kiss the sea –
15   What is all this sweet work worth
If thou kiss not me?

Repetition of "mingle" emphasises how everything in nature is united.

Dash creates a pause which emphasises the question at the end of the stanza.

Use of physical language hints at his frustration that he can't "kiss" and "clasp" his lover.

The narrator claims that his loved one's lack of love towards him goes against God's law and is therefore unforgivable.

The mirrored repetition of "kiss" and "clasp" reflects the narrator's belief that humans should mirror nature.

The final line in each stanza is monosyllabic and only has five syllables — this increases the impact of the questions and makes them stand out. They're separated from the rest of the poem, just as the narrator is separated from his lover.

The narrator questions the point of the world if his lover doesn't love him — this suggests that love gives life meaning. This question can also be seen as hyperbole — he might be deliberately going over the top to try to persuade her.

POEM DICTIONARY
fountains — natural springs
law divine — a law of God which can't be changed by man
thine — yours
disdain'd — looked down on or scorned

Percy Bysshe Shelley

Shelley (1792-1822) wrote this poem in 1820. He was a Romantic poet — Romanticism was an artistic and literary movement in the eighteenth and nineteenth centuries which put emphasis on emotion and nature.

You've got to know what the poem's about

1) The narrator is addressing a woman — he's trying to persuade her to be with him romantically.

2) The narrator gives examples to show how everything in nature is connected in an intimate and loving way. He believes that this is God's law and that this law should be obeyed.

3) He asks the woman he's addressing why she's ignoring God's law by refusing to have a loving relationship with him. He finally questions what use all the bonds in nature are if he can't be with her.

Learn about the form, structure and language

1) **FORM** — The poem is short and apparently simple — the narrator believes that what he's saying is a simple truth. The poem has a regular ABAB rhyme scheme, but two lines in each stanza don't fully rhyme — this reflects the way that all of nature is in harmony except for the narrator and his loved one.

2) **STRUCTURE** — The poem is tightly structured to be persuasive. The narrator uses the majority of each stanza to build up evidence to support his argument that everything in nature is supposed to come together. He uses a short line at the end of each stanza to ask a rhetorical question — this line stands out from the rest of the stanza, which emphasises the contrast between nature and the narrator's situation.

3) **LANGUAGE ABOUT NATURE** — The narrator uses personification to show the natural world giving, receiving and benefitting from love — this emphasises his point that love itself is natural and necessary.

4) **REPETITION** — Repetition is used to show how everything in nature repeatedly connects with everything else. Repeating words such as "mingle", "kiss" and "clasp" emphasises the physical relationship he wants.

5) **RELIGIOUS LANGUAGE** — Language to do with God suggests that love isn't just natural, it's also godly.

Remember the feelings and attitudes in the poem

1) **LONGING** — The narrator longs for love. He's frustrated that his love isn't returned when he sees all the bonds that exist in nature.

2) **PLAYFULNESS** — The poem can also be read in a playful way — the narrator oversimplifies the idea that because things in nature come together, he and the woman he wants should also come together.

"The tornado rips the trees to shreds"... one line that didn't make the final cut.

Go a step further and give a personal response

Have a go at answering these questions to help you come up with your own ideas about the poem:

Q1.   Why do you think the narrator refers to a "law divine"?

Q2.   How does the speaker try to make his argument persuasive?

Q3.   What do you think the narrator's main emotion is in this poem? Explain your answer.

Nature, longing...

'Winter Swans' is another poem that uses natural imagery to express love. You could also compare the sense of longing in this poem with the desire and frustration in 'Porphyria's Lover' and 'The Farmer's Bride'.

Section One — The Poems

Porphyria's Lover

Pathetic fallacy creates a threatening, ominous atmosphere.

Sets Tone

This description makes Porphyria seem almost magical.

Poetic Invers.

Repetition of "And" emphasises the calm way he's chronologically recounting the events leading up to her murder.

His passivity is strange — he doesn't speak and lets Porphyria arrange his body.

"Murmuring" could suggest her tone is flirtatious, or that she doesn't really mean what she says.

The narrator is critical of Porphyria's lack of commitment to him. She may be from a higher social class than him — this situation could be difficult for her as her family might not approve of the relationship.

First time in the poem that the speaker takes action — signals a shift in the balance of passivity and activity between Porphyria and the speaker.

She's come to be with him tonight and he's convinced she loves him, so he wants to preserve the moment.

This is clearly not true — the reader now has reason to question everything he's been saying.

Seems unlikely that her eyes are laughing, so maybe her eyes weren't "Happy and proud" in line 32 either.

He believes her red face (as a result of being strangled) is actually a blush from his passionate kiss — this shows that he's deranged.

Was 'she' earlier

He describes her as "it" — she's just an object to him now.

Objectifying

This is disturbing — the reader realises that she's been dead for the whole poem.

POEM DICTIONARY
vex — annoy
dissever — break off
prevail — win through
tress — a long lock of hair

The rain set early in tonight,
The sullen wind was soon awake,
It tore the elm-tops down for spite,
And did its worst to vex the lake:
5   I listened with heart fit to break.
When glided in Porphyria; straight
She shut the cold out and the storm,
And kneeled and made the cheerless grate
Blaze up, and all the cottage warm;
10 Which done, she rose, and from her form
Withdrew the dripping cloak and shawl,
And laid her soiled gloves by, untied
Her hat and let the damp hair fall,
And, last, she sat down by my side
15 And called me. When no voice replied,
She put my arm about her waist,
And made her smooth white shoulder bare,
And all her yellow hair displaced,
And, stooping, made my cheek lie there,
20 And spread, o'er all, her yellow hair,
Murmuring how she loved me – she
Too weak, for all her heart's endeavour,
To set its struggling passion free
From pride, and vainer ties dissever,
25 And give herself to me for ever.
But passion sometimes would prevail,
Nor could tonight's gay feast restrain
A sudden thought of one so pale
For love of her, and all in vain:
30 So, she was come through wind and rain.
Be sure I looked up at her eyes
Happy and proud; at last I knew
Porphyria worshipped me; surprise
Made my heart swell, and still it grew
35 While I debated what to do.
That moment she was mine, mine, fair,
Perfectly pure and good: I found
A thing to do, and all her hair
In one long yellow string I wound
40 Three times her little throat around,
And strangled her. No pain felt she;
I am quite sure she felt no pain.
As a shut bud that holds a bee,
I warily oped her lids: again
45 Laughed the blue eyes without a stain.
And I untightened next the tress
About her neck; her cheek once more
Blushed bright beneath my burning kiss:
I propped her head up as before,
50 Only, this time my shoulder bore
Her head, which droops upon it still:
The smiling rosy little head,
So glad it has its utmost will,
That all it scorned at once is fled,
55 And I, its love, am gained instead!
Porphyria's love: she guessed not how
Her darling one wish would be heard.
And thus we sit together now,
And all night long we have not stirred,
60 And yet God has not said a word!

This shows how the narrator is emotionally at breaking point and hints at his mental instability.

Porphyria seems to be a powerful, positive force in the speaker's life. Her actions contrast with the miserable weather.

Enjambment creates unusual line breaks that reflect the speaker's unstable mental state.

Female sexuality was repressed in Victorian times, but Porphyria is openly flaunting hers. Women who behaved like this were often labelled 'fallen women' — the use of the word "fall" draws attention to how Porphyria's behaviour would have been seen as sinful.

Repetition of "yellow hair" shows his obsession with it. It foreshadows his using it to strangle her later in the poem.

She's left some kind of party to see him — this could show how much she wants to see him, but also hints that he isn't part of her social activities.

He wants to be loved by her and to have power over her.

The repetition of "mine" is disturbing and suspicious — it emphasises how he wants to possess her.

This description of the murder is shocking because it's unexpected and matter-of-fact — there's no change in rhythm.

Caesura emphasises the sudden and final nature of this action.

Simile suggests that he is afraid of something when he opens her eyelids.

Ambiguity — this could mean there's no evidence of his sin, that he thinks she doesn't blame him for murdering her, or that there's no stain on her honour because she didn't have sex with him.

Juxtaposition shows the narrator's love for Porphyria is passionate but also destructive.

& + context
Priv. Sph.
use for
structure

Reversal of earlier in the poem — he's now active and Porphyria is passive.

Flower imagery reflects her beauty, but also depicts the speaker's foolishness — flowers droop, just as this perfect moment will not last.

Ambiguity — could be surprised that he hasn't been punished, or perhaps he doesn't believe that he's committed a sin at all.

Robert Browning

Robert Browning (1812-1889) was born in Camberwell, Surrey. He published 'Porphyria's Lover' in 1836. Porphyria is a disease that can result in madness — I'll leave you to decide whether that's significant or not...

You've got to know what the poem's about

1) A man sits in his <u>cold</u> cottage on a <u>stormy</u> night. Porphyria, his lover, arrives and makes the cottage <u>warm</u> and <u>comfortable</u>, before sitting down <u>next</u> to him.

2) He <u>ignores</u> her while she's flirting with him — he seems <u>upset</u> with her. However, he <u>decides</u> that she <u>loves</u> him and that she <u>belongs</u> to him — he wants to <u>preserve</u> the moment, so he <u>strangles</u> her with her own <u>hair</u>. It's clear that the speaker is <u>mentally disturbed</u>.

3) He opens her eyes and spends the rest of the night <u>sitting</u> with her dead <u>body</u>.

Learn about the form, structure and language

1) **FORM** — The poem is a <u>dramatic monologue</u>. The <u>asymmetrical</u> rhyme scheme (ABABB) and <u>enjambment</u> suggest that the speaker is <u>unstable</u>. However, the <u>regular rhythm</u> of the poem reflects his <u>calmness</u>. Porphyria has <u>no voice</u> in the poem — the speaker <u>projects</u> his own <u>thoughts</u> and <u>feelings</u> onto her in life and in death.

2) **STRUCTURE** — Events in the poem <u>mirror</u> each other. In the first half of the poem, Porphyria is <u>active</u> and <u>dominant</u> while her lover is <u>passive</u>, which is shown by the way she rests <u>his head</u> on <u>her shoulder</u>. These positions are <u>reversed</u> when the speaker <u>kills</u> her — afterwards he places <u>her head</u> on <u>his shoulder</u>.

3) **LANGUAGE OF POSSESSION** — The speaker wants Porphyria to <u>belong</u> to him "<u>for ever</u>", but he believes that her "<u>pride</u>" and "<u>vainer ties</u>" (possibly meaning her higher social status) are stopping her from being with him. He is <u>desperate</u> to possess her, and in death she becomes his <u>object</u>.

4) **LANGUAGE OF LOVE AND VIOLENCE** — The speaker combines <u>love</u> and <u>violence</u> to reflect the <u>troubled</u> and <u>destructive</u> nature of his love — e.g. "<u>heart fit to break</u>" and "<u>burning kiss</u>".

Remember the feelings and attitudes in the poem

1) MADNESS — It becomes clear that the speaker is <u>delusional</u> — he believes that Porphyria <u>wants</u> to be murdered so she can be with him <u>forever</u>, so his <u>reliability</u> throughout the poem has to be <u>questioned</u>.

2) PASSIVITY — The first half of the poem describes Porphyria's <u>actions</u> whilst her lover is <u>passive</u>. However, by killing her, the narrator makes Porphyria <u>completely passive</u>. She also seems passive <u>during</u> her murder — perhaps the narrator <u>chose</u> not to report any <u>struggle</u>, because to him it was a <u>perfect</u> moment.

3) SIN — The speaker comments that God <u>hasn't punished</u> him for the murder — he either believes that he's had a <u>lucky escape</u>, or, more worryingly, that he <u>hasn't committed a sin</u>. Porphyria's actions could also be seen as sinful — Victorians would have viewed a woman sneaking off to see her lover as <u>immoral</u>.

Go a step further and give a personal response

Have a go at <u>answering</u> these <u>questions</u> to help you come up with <u>your own ideas</u> about the poem:

Q1.   Why do you think the speaker murders his lover?

Q2.   Find an example of repetition in the poem. What effect does it have?

Q3.   Do you think Porphyria loves the speaker? Does he love her? Explain your answers.

Longing, destructive love, death...
Longing is also presented as potentially destructive in the 'The Farmer's Bride'. You could look at 'Sonnet 29' if you're writing about longing, or 'Eden Rock' to explore the idea of love enduring beyond death.

8

Sonnet 29 — 'I think of thee!'

The narrator addresses her lover directly, which makes the poem seem more personal.

Exclamation mark emphasises the pleasure she takes in thinking about him.

Natural imagery shows how her thoughts focus on him like a vine wraps around a tree — her thoughts are constantly growing and developing.

Metaphor — the narrator is the "wild vines" and her lover is the "tree". This is emphasised by the internal rhyme of "thee" and "tree".

Suggests her love for him is extensive.

Her thoughts threaten to stop her from seeing him as he really is.

Suggests the vines are inferior to the tree — her thoughts about her lover are inferior to the man himself.

Caesura creates a turning point (volta) in the poem.

Imperatives and alliteration emphasise how much she wants him to act.

Sibilant sounds reflect the rustling of the tree's leaves.

The weight of her thoughts emphasises how much she thinks about him.

Possibly an erotic reference.

Plosive sound marks the conclusion of her argument — she wants him to understand how much she enjoys being with him.

Use of three different words to describe the way his presence replaces her thoughts emphasises her excitement. Caesura contributes to the dramatic effect.

Reversal of the first line highlights the difference between thinking about him and being with him.

She doesn't have to think about him when she's with him — he's better than anything she's capable of imagining.

Rhymes him with himself — this shows her obsession with him.

I think of thee! – my thoughts do twine and bud
About thee, as wild vines, about a tree,
Put out broad leaves, and soon there's nought to see
Except the straggling green which hides the wood.
5　Yet, O my palm-tree, be it understood
I will not have my thoughts instead of thee
Who art dearer, better! Rather, instantly
Renew thy presence; as a strong tree should,
Rustle thy boughs and set thy trunk all bare,
10　And let these bands of greenery which insphere thee
Drop heavily down, – burst, shattered, everywhere!
Because, in this deep joy to see and hear thee
And breathe within thy shadow a new air,
I do not think of thee – I am too near thee.

POEM DICTIONARY
twine — wind around something
straggling — not orderly
insphere — completely enclose

Elizabeth Barrett Browning

Elizabeth Barrett Browning (1806-1861) was born in County Durham. She wrote this poem in 1845-46 as part of a series of sonnets about her future husband, Robert Browning, called *Sonnets from the Portuguese*.

You've got to know what the poem's about

1) The narrator tells her lover how much she <u>thinks</u> about him when they're <u>not together</u>. She's <u>worried</u> that her thoughts will <u>obscure</u> the reality of what he's actually like.

2) However, she reassures him that her <u>thoughts</u> do not <u>compare</u> to the <u>reality</u> of him. She wants him to be a <u>strong presence</u> in her life and to be <u>with him</u> rather than just <u>thinking about</u> him.

Learn about the form, structure and language

1) **FORM** — Sonnet form is traditionally used for <u>love</u> poetry. This sonnet is loosely written in the <u>Petrarchan form</u>, with eight lines (an <u>octave</u>) followed by six lines (a <u>sestet</u>) — the octave usually presents a <u>problem</u> and the sestet provides a <u>solution</u>. However, in this poem, the solution arrives in the <u>middle</u> of <u>line 7</u> — having it come <u>early</u> and in the <u>middle</u> of a line reflects the narrator's <u>impatience</u> to see her lover.

2) **STRUCTURE** — The <u>transition</u> from the problem to the solution reflects the <u>difference</u> between the narrator <u>thinking</u> about her lover and being <u>with him</u>. This is emphasised by the <u>reversal</u> of the first and last lines — in the <u>first</u> line, the narrator says "<u>I think of thee!</u>", but by the end of the poem, she imagines that when she's with her lover, she'll no longer think of him because she'll be "<u>too near</u>" him.

3) **LANGUAGE ABOUT NATURE** — The narrator uses an <u>extended metaphor</u> throughout the poem — the narrator's lover is a <u>tree</u> and her thoughts are "<u>wild vines</u>" which <u>cover</u> him. This shows how her thoughts are <u>constantly growing</u> and <u>unrestrained</u>. The image of the tree <u>casting off</u> the vines reflects how she wants her lover to be a <u>strong</u>, <u>permanent</u> part of her life.

4) **EXCITED LANGUAGE** — The use of <u>exclamation marks</u> shows how the narrator takes <u>joy</u> in thinking about her lover and feels <u>excitement</u> at the thought of being with him. <u>Plosive</u> sounds and <u>dynamic verbs</u> emphasise how she much she wants to be <u>with</u> him.

Remember the feelings and attitudes in the poem

1) **LONGING** — The narrator longs to be <u>with</u> her lover instead of just <u>thinking</u> about him.

2) **INTENSITY** — She thinks about her lover <u>all the time</u> when they're apart. Her language is <u>forceful</u> — she uses imperatives which almost <u>order</u> him to be with her.

3) **CELEBRATION** — She takes <u>pleasure</u> in her feelings of love for him — she <u>enjoys</u> the way her thoughts envelop him, but she takes even <u>greater joy</u> in the thought of him being a <u>physical presence</u> in her life.

Maybe her feelings for him weren't as strong as she thought...

Go a step further and give a personal response

Have a go at <u>answering</u> these <u>questions</u> to help you come up with <u>your own ideas</u> about the poem:

Q1.   Why do you think the narrator compares her lover to a tree?

Q2.   Do you get the impression that her love is returned?

Q3.   What do you think the narrator means by "new air" in line 13?

Fulfilment, nature, distance, longing...

Consider how relationships are presented as fulfilling in 'Singh Song!' and 'Climbing My Grandfather'. Natural imagery is also used to show distance in a relationship in 'Letters From Yorkshire' and 'Winter Swans'.

Neutral Tones

The sun is drained of warmth and colour — reflects how the love has drained from their relationship.

Lack of physical movement contributes to lifeless atmosphere.

Weather reflects their feelings — they're emotionally cold towards each other.

Imagines that God has scolded the sun. This adds to the bleak mood of the poem, and hints that the narrator sees everything in a negative way.

Alliteration emphasises how the leaves are still and unmoving.

In love poems, eyes are traditionally shown to be a positive feature, but they're shown negatively here.

Enjambment mimics how her eyes move over his face. The words "rove" and "Over" look and sound similar, which reflects the boredom she feels.

Alliteration and personification emphasises this impression of suffering — the lifeless ground reflects their dying relationship.

The leaves are from an ash tree, but this also links to ash from a fire — their relationship has burnt out.

Game imagery — love should be fun and playful, but theirs became "tedious" and they "lost".

We stood by a pond that winter day,
And the sun was white, as though chidden of God,
And a few leaves lay on the starving sod;
 — They had fallen from an ash, and were grey.

5 Your eyes on me were as eyes that rove
Over tedious riddles of years ago;
And some words played between us to and fro
 On which lost the more by our love.

The smile on your mouth was the deadest thing
10 Alive enough to have strength to die;
And a grin of bitterness swept thereby
 Like an ominous bird a-wing…

Since then, keen lessons that love deceives,
And wrings with wrong, have shaped to me
15 Your face, and the God-curst sun, and a tree,
 And a pond edged with greyish leaves.

Oxymoron — a smile shouldn't be dead. This emphasises her complete lack of feeling towards him.

She chose to let her smile die — maybe she chose to let the love between them die too.

Imagery of a bird flying away suggests the end of the relationship.

Ellipsis represents the time when the relationship came to an end, in the time that passes between stanzas 3 and 4.

"keen" means sharp or strong — these lessons have been painful.

He makes a pessimistic generalisation that all love is deceptive.

Alliteration emphasises his pain and anguish.

Other experiences of deceitful love remind him of this incident by the pond — perhaps it was the first time he experienced it.

Poem begins and ends by the pond — this shows how the memory of that day still affects him.

The "t" in "curst" is a harsher sound than "chidden" in the first stanza — this hints that the narrator has become more bitter over time.

The leaves are grey because they're rotting — this reflects how their love has decayed. The repetition of this colour from the first stanza emphasises the decay.

POEM DICTIONARY
chidden — scolded
sod — grass-covered earth
rove — wander
thereby — by
a-wing — flying
wrings — squeezes or twists forcefully
curst — cursed

Thomas Hardy

Thomas Hardy (1840-1928) was born in Dorset. 'Neutral Tones' was written in 1867 and published in 1898 as part of his *Wessex Poems and Other Verses* collection. Much of his work is regarded as pessimistic and bleak.

You've got to know what the poem's about

1) The narrator <u>remembers</u> a day when he and his lover stood by a pond. It's an <u>unpleasant</u> memory — it's clear that their relationship was <u>failing</u> and about to come to an <u>end</u>.

2) He describes his lover's <u>behaviour</u> — he seems to believe that she found him <u>boring</u> and had fallen <u>out of love</u> with him.

3) Whenever he's been hurt by love since, he <u>remembers</u> that day by the pond.

Learn about the form, structure and language

1) **FORM** — The poem is written from the point of view of a man addressing a <u>past lover</u>. The <u>first</u> and <u>last</u> lines of each stanza <u>rhyme</u> — this reflects how the <u>memory</u> of a <u>past</u> experience returns to affect the narrator in the <u>present</u>. The <u>indented final line</u> of each stanza <u>slows</u> the pace of the poem by creating a <u>pause</u> — this hints at his <u>sadness</u> that the relationship failed.

2) **STRUCTURE** — The first three stanzas centre around a specific <u>memory</u>, then there's a <u>time jump</u> to the final stanza where the narrator <u>reflects</u> on love in general. The poem <u>ends</u> where it <u>began</u>, with the image of a <u>pond</u> — this <u>cyclical structure</u> represents how he's been repeatedly <u>hurt</u> by love <u>since</u> that day by the pond, and the way that these experiences always <u>remind</u> him of that day.

3) **LANGUAGE ABOUT SUFFERING** — Although the 'neutral' tone of the poem is <u>never broken</u>, it's clear that the narrator feels <u>strong emotions</u> about that day by the pond — he uses language associated with <u>pain</u>, <u>death</u> and <u>punishment</u>, which shows that he's <u>hurt</u> by what happened.

4) **LANGUAGE ABOUT LIFELESSNESS** — The '<u>neutral</u>' <u>tone</u> shows the <u>lack of love</u> between the narrator and his lover, and the <u>pessimistic</u> way the narrator now feels about love in general. The <u>death</u> of their relationship and his <u>lack of hope</u> are reflected in the landscape — it's <u>bleak</u>, <u>decaying</u> and <u>cold</u>.

Remember the feelings and attitudes in the poem

1) **BITTERNESS** — The narrator feels <u>bitter</u> about the <u>breakdown</u> of his relationship — he <u>resents</u> the <u>lack</u> of real <u>emotion</u> behind his lover's smile and the way she seemed <u>bored</u> of him.

2) **PESSIMISM** — Other negative experiences of love since the relationship described in the poem have only <u>confirmed</u> his pessimistic view of love. The <u>bleak</u> mood and <u>colourless</u> setting show that there's a <u>lack of hope</u> everywhere, even in <u>nature</u>.

Go a step further and give a personal response

Have a go at <u>answering</u> these <u>questions</u> to help you come up with <u>your own ideas</u> about the poem:

Q1. Do you think the narrator blames his lover for the end of their relationship? Why/ Why not?

Q2. How is time used in the poem?

Q3. What do you think the title of the poem refers to?

Death, nature, memory...

'Winter Swans' and 'The Farmer's Bride' also use imagery of nature to reflect troubled relationships. The power of memory is significant in 'Eden Rock', but there it is a positive rather than a negative force.

The Farmer's Bride

Three Summers since I chose a maid,
Too young maybe – but more's to do
At harvest-time than bide and woo.
    When us was wed she turned afraid
5 Of love and me and all things human;
Like the shut of a winter's day
Her smile went out, and 'twasn't a woman –
    More like a little frightened fay.
        One night, in the Fall, she runned away.

10 'Out 'mong the sheep, her be,' they said,
Should properly have been abed;
But sure enough she wasn't there
Lying awake with her wide brown stare.
    So over seven-acre field and up-along across the down
15 We chased her, flying like a hare
    Before our lanterns. To Church-Town
All in a shiver and a scare
We caught her, fetched her home at last
    And turned the key upon her, fast.

20 She does the work about the house
As well as most, but like a mouse:
    Happy enough to chat and play
    With birds and rabbits and such as they,
    So long as men-folk keep away.
25 'Not near, not near!' her eyes beseech
When one of us comes within reach.
    The women say that beasts in stall
    Look round like children at her call.
    I've hardly heard her speak at all.

30 Shy as a leveret, swift as he,
Straight and slight as a young larch tree,
Sweet as the first wild violets, she,
To her wild self. But what to me?

The short days shorten and the oaks are brown,
35   The blue smoke rises to the low grey sky,
One leaf in the still air falls slowly down,
    A magpie's spotted feathers lie
On the black earth spread white with rime,
The berries redden up to Christmas-time.
40   What's Christmas-time without there be
    Some other in the house than we!

    She sleeps up in the attic there
    Alone, poor maid. 'Tis but a stair
Betwixt us. Oh! my God! the down,
45 The soft young down of her; the brown,
The brown of her – her eyes, her hair, her hair!

Annotations

She wasn't afraid until after they were married — this could hint that he's responsible for her fear in some way.

Shows system of patriarchy (male authority over women) — suggests she didn't have much choice about their marriage. This is reflected in the title — it sounds like she belongs to him.

Hints that the farmer had a practical and unromantic approach to marriage.

Simile shows how sudden this change was — winter days go dark very quickly.

Anticipates the comparisons to animals that follow. It's a strong statement, but the source of this fear is a mystery.

Hunting imagery — suggests her terror.

Dialect of the farmer — we can hear his voice, and it's one he shares with his community.

Her fear is expressed physically, like a hunted animal — "scare" is rhymed with "hare", which emphasises the comparison.

The rhyming couplet emphasises the decisive action of locking her away and makes it sound sinister.

The whole village seems to be involved — this adds to the sense that she's being hunted.

The change to the present tense emphasises his resigned, baffled tone. She's a fairly good housewife — she does what is expected of her in the relationship, apart from loving her husband.

She is nearly silent and only speaks to animals. She sounds withdrawn and depressed.

She's linked with small prey animals to show her vulnerability.

Links back to the imagery of the hunt — she still feels under threat.

Simile shows that the farm animals trust her and look to her for care — may suggest he's jealous of them.

Rhyming triplet emphasises the narrator's frustration at his wife's behaviour.

Has connotations both of an unspoilt freedom and of a rejection of people.

Repeated use of sibilant sounds emphasises her link with nature. The irregularity of this short stanza could reflect the farmer's growing agitation by this link and his unfulfilled desire for her.

Sad, lonely image — symbolises his sinking hope that she will ever come to him freely.

Rhetorical question — breaks his happier thoughts of her in springtime and takes him back to the winter scene.

Christmas is about the birth of a child — they have no children because of her refusal of him.

Winter is used to suggest the decay and death of his hopes.

He is aware of her physical closeness, adding to his frustration.

Sounds sympathetic but also suggests that she's still a virgin — a "maid" is a young, unmarried girl.

Animal-like descriptions show his desire for her — even though these qualities are also the source of his frustration. Internal rhyme of "brown" and "down" emphasises his desire and frustration.

Frantic-sounding repetition of the half-rhyme "her hair" — he's breaking down and losing control.

POEM DICTIONARY
bide — wait
woo — try to win someone's love
fay — a fairy
leveret — a young hare
rime — frost

Charlotte Mew

Mew (1869-1928) published this poem in 1912. She is thought to have been homosexual, at a time when homosexuality wasn't accepted by society. This might explain the tone of longing and frustration in the poem...

You've got to know what the poem's about

1) A farmer has been married for three years but his bride is frightened of him and other men.

2) In the poem he tells the story of how the relationship went wrong.
He doesn't question whether he has any responsibility for his wife's fear.

3) He finds her rejection of him almost unbearable, but he expresses his thoughts in a fairly matter-of-fact way. He desires his wife, and by the end it seems he may be struggling to resist taking her by force.

Learn about the form, structure and language

1) **FORM** — The poem is a dramatic monologue, mostly in iambic tetrameter, with a rhyme scheme that varies through the poem. This helps give the poem a strong rhythm that drives the narrative forward without becoming predictable. It's written entirely from the farmer's point of view — his wife has no voice.

2) **STRUCTURE** — The farmer tells the story of the marriage failing through the first two stanzas, then goes on to discuss how his wife is now, how he feels towards her, his sadness and his desire.

3) **DIALECT** — The poem contains many dialect words, which help to give a strong sense of the farmer's character. We can hear his voice in his language and in his grammar — this adds to the drama as it helps us picture the people involved.

4) **LANGUAGE ABOUT NATURE** — The farmer mainly uses imagery taken from the natural world. This reflects his identity, whilst his descriptions of his wife link her to images of nature and wildness. In the second stanza she is likened to a hunted hare.

Remember the feelings and attitudes in the poem

"Maybe you should just talk to the guy — tell him how you feel."

1) **FRUSTRATION** — He wants to have a sexual relationship with her and have children, but she's unwilling and uncommunicative.

2) **DESIRE** — The farmer is clearly attracted to his wife. This is expressed both in the imagery he uses to describe her and the way he breaks down at the end of the poem.

3) **FEAR** — The farmer's wife is clearly afraid. There is also a sense of foreboding — the farmer is struggling to control his desire for her, and there is little to suggest that there will be a happy ending for the married couple.

Go a step further and give a personal response

Have a go at answering these questions to help you come up with your own ideas about the poem:

Q1.   How far do you blame the farmer for his wife's behaviour?

Q2.   How does the poet use the different seasons to describe the relationship?

Q3.   To what extent would you describe 'The Farmer's Bride' as a love poem?

Desire, distance, nature...

Compare the farmer's physical desire with that of the speakers in 'Porphyria's Lover' and 'Love's Philosophy'. You could also look at the emotional distance in 'Neutral Tones' and the physical distance in 'Sonnet 29'.

Walking Away

New boundaries are also being drawn between father and son, with the son's newfound independence.

He remembers the exact day — it's an important memory.

Transition from summer to autumn reflects the transition in the son's life.

Negative simile — a satellite isn't meant to fall out of orbit, and to drift away makes the son sound helpless and in danger. The simile also emphasises how the father has stopped being at the centre of his son's life.

Enjambment puts the unexpected word "Wrenched" at the start of the line, which emphasises it. This reflects how the father found the separation sudden and painful.

It is eighteen years ago, almost to the day –
A sunny day with the leaves just turning,
The touch-lines new-ruled – since I watched you play
Your first game of football, then, like a satellite
5 Wrenched from its orbit, go drifting away

Enjambment highlights the way the boy turns away from his father to follow the other boys.

Suggests a hostile place — father worries his son won't survive without his protection.

Behind a scatter of boys. I can see
You walking away from me towards the school
With the pathos of a half-fledged thing set free
Into a wilderness, the gait of one
10 Who finds no path where the path should be.

Bird metaphor used to show the father's concern that his son isn't ready.

Repetition of "path" emphasises that the father is desperate for his son to find the right way in life and that he sees him as helpless.

"eddying" is a natural image that compares the son to something moving in a current of air or water — this reflects his uncertainty and lack of control.

That hesitant figure, eddying away
Like a winged seed loosened from its parent stem,
Has something I never quite grasp to convey
About nature's give-and-take – the small, the scorching
15 Ordeals which fire one's irresolute clay.

Experiences of growing up are painful.

Natural simile contrasts with the satellite simile in stanza 1 — "loosened" is less painful and forced than "Wrenched". This shows how the father is coming to terms with what happened and understands that it's natural.

Fire turns clay into a pot — difficult experiences of growing up turn children into independent people.

I have had worse partings, but none that so
Gnaws at my mind still. Perhaps it is roughly
Saying what God alone could perfectly show –
How selfhood begins with a walking away,
20 And love is proved in the letting go.

"Gnaws" is animalistic and vicious — the father is still affected by seeing his son go through the tough process of growing up.

The change to a more steady rhythm underlines how the father has come to a philosophical understanding — the son has to walk away from his father to find his own identity, and the father proves his love for his son by letting him go.

Religious imagery — in the Bible, God let go of Jesus, his only son, when Jesus came to Earth and was crucified. He did this to show humans that he loved them. That "God alone" could do it shows how difficult it is.

POEM DICTIONARY
pathos — something that creates feelings of pity
half-fledged — describes a young bird that doesn't have all its
    adult feathers. A bird that isn't fully fledged is unable to fly
gait — the way someone walks
eddying — air or water moving in a circular motion
irresolute — uncertain

C. Day Lewis

Cecil Day Lewis (1904-1972) was born in Ireland and studied at Oxford. 'Walking Away' was published in 1962 and was dedicated to his first son, Sean. Day Lewis was Poet Laureate from 1968 until his death in 1972.

You've got to know what the poem's about

1) A father remembers watching his son play his <u>first</u> game of football, possibly on his first day at <u>school</u>. The father feels <u>worried</u> about his son as he watches him walk <u>uncertainly</u> away from him.

2) The memory of that day still <u>deeply</u> affects the father <u>eighteen years later</u>. However, he comes to an <u>understanding</u> that this is a <u>natural process</u> that all children and parents must go through — every child has to experience the difficult process of gaining <u>independence</u>, and every parent has to <u>let go</u>.

Learn about the form, structure and language

1) **FORM** — The poem has a <u>first-person</u> narrator — this emphasises that it's talking about <u>personal experiences</u>. The use of <u>enjambment</u> and <u>caesura</u> contributes to the <u>rhythm</u> of the poem, which sounds like <u>natural speech</u>. The regular <u>ABACA</u> rhyme scheme reflects the <u>steadiness</u> of the father's <u>parental love</u>, and the <u>repetition</u> of the '<u>A</u>' rhyme reflects how the memory of that day <u>continues</u> to affect him years later.

2) **STRUCTURE** — In the <u>first two</u> stanzas the narrator talks about the <u>memory</u>. In the <u>final two</u> stanzas, he <u>reflects</u> on how the memory still <u>pains</u> him. The <u>final two lines</u> of the poem form a sort of <u>conclusion</u> — he <u>understands</u> that whilst it was a <u>painful</u> event, it was a <u>necessary</u> part of his son's <u>development</u>.

3) **NATURAL IMAGERY** — Natural imagery is used to show the father's growing <u>understanding</u> that his son walking away from him is <u>natural</u>, but also that he remains <u>concerned</u> about him. He compares his son to a "<u>half-fledged</u>" bird out in the "<u>wilderness</u>" — he's <u>worried</u> because he sees his son as <u>vulnerable</u>.

4) **LANGUAGE ABOUT PAIN** — Verbs such as "<u>Wrenched</u>", "<u>scorching</u>" and "<u>Gnaws</u>" show how the process is <u>traumatic</u> for the father as well as <u>difficult</u> for the son.

Remember the feelings and attitudes in the poem

1) **PROTECTIVENESS** — The father sees his son as vulnerable, but understands that he <u>can't protect</u> him forever — he now has to show his <u>love</u> for his son by letting him gain some <u>independence</u>.

2) **LOSS** — There's a feeling of <u>loss</u> and sadness throughout the poem, but also the <u>understanding</u> that "walking away" is a <u>natural</u> part of growing up. It's not a <u>permanent parting</u>, their relationship is just being <u>redefined</u>.

3) **REFLECTION** — The father is <u>philosophical</u> about the <u>relationship</u> between parents and their children — although his son leaving his protection was <u>painful</u>, he understands that it was <u>necessary</u> for both of them.

Go a step further and give a personal response

Have a go at <u>answering</u> these <u>questions</u> to help you come up with <u>your own ideas</u> about the poem:

Q1.   Why do you think the speaker addresses his son directly (e.g. "I watched you play")?

Q2.   How is natural imagery used to show the father's feelings about his son walking away?

Q3.   The father says the memory still "Gnaws" at his mind. Why do you think this is?

KEY THEMES *Family relationships, getting older, memory...*

'Climbing My Grandfather' also features a close, significant family relationship. Have a look at 'Mother, Any Distance' to consider how children growing up affects their parents, or write about memory in 'Eden Rock'.

Section One — The Poems

Letters From Yorkshire

He works closely with the land.

Alliteration emphasises that it's a repetitive, ordinary action.

He's connected with nature and its cycles.

While the narrator might romanticise this man's life, for him it's just reality. This could also be a description of their relationship.

Use of caesura shifts the focus from his ordinary actions to personification. The personification shows the delight he feels.

In February, digging his garden, planting potatoes,
he saw the first lapwings return and came
indoors to write to me, his knuckles singing

Monosyllabic words reflect his simple way of life.

The computer shows the contrast between their lifestyles and professions — "blank screen" sounds lifeless and empty compared to his "singing" knuckles.

as they reddened in the warmth.
5   It's not romance, simply how things are.
You out there, in the cold, seeing the seasons

Enjambment imitates the changing seasons.

Figurative language creates a contrast between her feeding words and him feeding people with his potatoes. Her actions seem artificial compared to his experiences of nature.

Description of mundane, physical tasks shows how he sees his life as ordinary, but also reiterates his connection with nature.

turning, me with my heartful of headlines
feeding words onto a blank screen.
Is your life more real because you dig and sow?

Rhetorical question in the middle stanza reflects how this issue is at the centre of what the poem is about.

Caesura introduces a contrasting perspective on his lifestyle — he wouldn't say that there's anything special about his life, but the narrator thinks there is.

10   You wouldn't say so, breaking ice on a waterbutt,
clearing a path through snow. Still, it's you
who sends me word of that other world

More natural than the words she writes. He writes to her about his day-to-day life and she romanticises it by describing it in terms of "air and light" — an almost magical description.

pouring air and light into an envelope. So that
at night, watching the same news in different houses,
15   our souls tap out messages across the icy miles.

Alliteration and assonance make these words sound similar, but they're also different — this reflects how his words make the speaker feel close to his world, but also remind her that she's distant from it.

Spiritual language shows they have a deep and meaningful connection.

Communication brings them together, despite the distance between them. Describing this distance as "icy" suggests that she dislikes being so far away from him.

Watching the same news hints that their lives aren't so different — this shared experience make her feel closer to him.

POEM DICTIONARY
lapwings — a type of bird usually found on farmland
waterbutt — an outdoor barrel which collects and stores rainwater

Maura Dooley

Maura Dooley was born in 1957 in Truro, Cornwall. She lived in Yorkshire for a few years before moving to London, where she's now a lecturer in Creative Writing. 'Letters From Yorkshire' was published in 2002.

You've got to know what the poem's about

1) A man is working in his garden. He sees his first lapwings of the season and writes to the narrator about it.

2) The narrator reflects on their different lives — the man lives in Yorkshire and spends time outside, whereas she lives a long way away, presumably in a city, and spends her time inside writing.

3) The narrator wonders if his life is more fulfilling because he's closer to nature. She feels as though he lives in a different world, but the letters he writes help her to feel connected to him and his way of life.

Learn about the form, structure and language

1) **FORM** — The poem is written in free verse, which makes the poem flow like natural speech or a letter. Enjambment allows lines and stanzas to flow into each other — this continuous movement reflects the way the seasons are constantly changing. The use of three-line stanzas instead of an even number of lines makes the poem look disjointed — this reflects how the narrator feels disconnected from the man.

2) **STRUCTURE** — In the first three stanzas, the narrator shows how she and the man live different lives. Despite this, it becomes clear in the final two stanzas that they have a deep connection.

3) **PHYSICAL VERBS** — A series of active verbs (e.g. "digging", "planting") describe the letter writer's physical work in his garden. They are ordinary but satisfying actions that emphasise his connection with nature.

4) **CONTRASTS** — The narrator presents her lifestyle as different to the letter writer's — he works outside while she sits at a computer. Whilst he sees his life as ordinary, she romanticises it and sees her own life as inferior. Alliteration emphasises the contrast between her "heartful of headlines" and his "seeing the seasons" — the word "headlines" sounds melodramatic and artificial compared to the natural "seasons".

5) **LANGUAGE ABOUT COMMUNICATION** — Communication bridges the distance between them and emphasises the things they have in common. Figurative language suggests their connection is almost spiritual.

Remember the feelings and attitudes in the poem

1) **APPRECIATION** — The narrator appreciates the man's way of life — she values his closeness to nature and how he experiences things that she doesn't in her everyday life.

2) **CONNECTION** — The narrator and the letter writer are close — it seems that he writes to her a lot about the little things that happen in his life that are important to him, such as seeing the lapwings.

3) **LONGING** — She seems to long for his lifestyle — she sees it as romantic and fulfilling.

"Wonder what he'd do if he saw us in his garden..."

Go a step further and give a personal response

Have a go at answering these questions to help you come up with your own ideas about the poem:

Q1.   Do you think the narrator dislikes her own life? Explain your answer.
Q2.   Describe your impression of the relationship between the narrator and the letter writer.
Q3.   Why do you think the poem is set in February?

Nature, longing, distance...

The narrator in 'Follower' also looks up to someone whose life is connected with nature, and longs to be like them. You could write about 'Sonnet 29' if you're looking at the impact of distance on relationships.

Section One — The Poems

Eden Rock

Eden Rock is a made-up, imaginary place. Eden was an image of paradise/heavenly place in religion. This reflects the utopian, ideal relationship that Charles has with his parents.

> The use of the present tense makes the scene he's describing feel more vivid.

> Vague description hints that this is an imagined scene.

> Biblical reference to the Garden of Eden. The Garden of Eden was a perfect place, which suggests that, for the narrator, this place with his parents is perfect and peaceful.

They are waiting for me somewhere beyond Eden Rock:
My father, twenty-five, in the same suit
Of Genuine Irish Tweed, his terrier Jack
Still two years old and trembling at his feet.

> The introductions to the two parents mirror each other — this reflects the closeness of their relationship.

> The narrator seems to take comfort in remembering specific things about his parents.

5 My mother, twenty-three, in a sprigged dress
Drawn at the waist, ribbon in her straw hat,
Has spread the stiff white cloth over the grass.
Her hair, the colour of wheat, takes on the light.

> Pure, heavenly colour.

> These beautiful details show how precious this memory of his mother is to the narrator.

> The detailed descriptions of these specific, ordinary things show their importance to the narrator and the affection he has for the way his parents did things.

> The light in his mother's hair is an angelic image.

Wheat is quite a golden colour which gives an angellic feel to the parents

She pours tea from a Thermos, the milk straight
10 From an old H.P. Sauce bottle, a screw
Of paper for a cork; slowly sets out
The same three plates, the tin cups painted blue.

> The actions of the mother and father are tranquil and peaceful.

> This hints at something otherworldly, in contrast with the ordinary descriptions of the first three stanzas — it is like a heavenly light. The three suns could also symbolise that their family of three has been reunited.

The sky whitens as if lit by three suns.
My mother shades her eyes and looks my way
15 Over the drifted stream. My father spins
A stone along the water. Leisurely,

> Caesurae slow the pace of the poem, which emphasises the feeling of peace.

> Enjambment creates a pause, which may imitate the leisurely way the narrator's parents beckon to him.

> Even the stream is peaceful. This suggests he'll have no trouble crossing it to get to his parents.

They beckon to me from the other bank.
I hear them call, "See where the stream-path is!
Crossing is not as hard as you might think."

> Possibly a metaphor for crossing into death.

20 I had not thought that it would be like this.

> The narrator's parents comfort and encourage him — a typical role of parents.

> Monosyllabic language creates a tone of child-like simplicity. The meaning of this last line is ambiguous — we don't know what "it" actually is. He may be referring to his preparing to be born or to die, or he may be talking about the afterlife itself.

Child-like language shows he wants to go back to childhood and live the idyllic life w/ both parents died/alive. Dad died when he was 7.

POEM DICTIONARY
Eden — the perfect garden in the Bible where Adam and Eve were said to have lived
Tweed — a woollen fabric, often with a checked pattern
sprigged — patterned with small bunches of flowers
Thermos — a brand of flask

Charles Causley

Charles Causley (1917-2003) was born in Launceston, Cornwall. An only child, Causley was only 7 when his father died. He may be talking about his own parents in 'Eden Rock', which was published in 1988.

You've got to know what the poem's about

1) The narrator imagines that his parents are both <u>young</u> again — his mother is <u>23</u> and his father is <u>25</u>. They're both on the bank of a <u>stream</u> and his mother is preparing a picnic — it's an <u>idyllic</u> scene.

2) The narrator is on the <u>opposite</u> bank to his parents, and they <u>encourage</u> him to cross the river to join them.

3) The setting may be based on a <u>real memory</u>, or it may be an <u>imagined</u> scene of the time <u>before</u> the narrator was <u>born</u> or when he's <u>near death</u> — his parents could be beckoning him to join them in <u>life</u>, or in the <u>afterlife</u>.

Learn about the form, structure and language

1) **FORM** — The poem is made up of <u>five stanzas</u>, mostly four <u>lines</u> long and nearly every line has <u>ten syllables</u> — this <u>regular</u> structure reflects the <u>steady</u> nature of the narrator's relationship with his parents. The <u>final line</u> is separated from the rest of the stanza — this could emphasise the narrator's current <u>separation</u> from his parents, or it could show that he has now <u>crossed</u> the stream and is looking at what's <u>beyond</u>. The poet mainly uses <u>half-rhymes</u>, which create a <u>gentle</u>, <u>natural rhythm</u>.

2) **STRUCTURE** — In the first <u>three stanzas</u> the narrator <u>affectionately</u> describes his <u>parents</u>, showing his <u>fondness</u> for them. In the <u>fourth</u> and <u>fifth</u> stanzas, his parents turn their <u>attention</u> to him and <u>encourage</u> him to <u>join</u> them.

3) **LANGUAGE ABOUT MEMORY** — The narrator uses <u>childhood memories</u> to create a <u>vivid</u> scene. The <u>beautiful</u> and <u>peaceful</u> descriptions of his parents reflect how <u>special</u> his childhood is to him.

4) **LANGUAGE ABOUT LIGHT** — References to <u>light</u> and the colour <u>white</u> may suggest a <u>heavenly</u> setting.

5) **LANGUAGE ABOUT ORDINARINESS** — <u>Specific details</u> such as the "H.P. Sauce bottle" show the narrator's <u>nostalgia</u> for the details of everyday life when he was a child. The use of ordinary language reflects how life was <u>simple</u> and <u>uncomplicated</u> back then and shows the narrator's <u>fondness</u> for this time.

Remember the feelings and attitudes in the poem

1) **DEEP AND LASTING BOND** — The parents have been <u>waiting</u> for their son. If the narrator is talking about death, he isn't <u>scared</u> — he'll be <u>reunited</u> with his parents, so it's just like going back to <u>childhood</u>.

2) **NOSTALGIA** — As the poet's father died when he was 7, the narrator's <u>affection</u> for the time when he and his parents were <u>together</u> as a family could <u>reflect</u> the poet's own <u>desire</u> to see his parents again.

3) **PEACEFULNESS** — There is a feeling of peace <u>throughout</u> the poem. This could reflect the narrator's <u>emotions</u> — he feels at peace when he thinks about his <u>parents</u> and imagines being <u>reunited</u> with them.

Go a step further and give a personal response

Have a go at <u>answering</u> these <u>questions</u> to help you come up with <u>your own ideas</u> about the poem:

Q1.   Why do you think the poet chose to call the place in the poem Eden Rock?

Q2.   How would you describe the mood of the narrator?

Q3.   Why do you think the last line is separate from the rest of the stanza?

Family relationships, memory, distance...

'Follower' also explores the close, lasting bonds of parent/child relationships. You could discuss the vivid childhood memories in 'Before You Were Mine' or how distance is overcome in 'Letters From Yorkshire'.

Section One — The Poems

Follower

The assonant long "o" sounds emphasise the broadness of his shoulders.

This simile shows that, just as sails harness the power of the wind, he harnesses the power of the horses and uses them to plough.

This verb suggests tough, physical work.

Onomatopoeia draws attention to his skill — he can control the powerful horses just by clicking his tongue.

My father worked with a horse-plough,
His shoulders globed like a full sail strung
Between the shafts and the furrow.
The horses strained at his clicking tongue.

Describing his father as an expert shows that he's technically skilled as well as strong. This short, blunt sentence and its position at the start of the line makes it a confident, inarguable statement.

Repetition of the hard-sounding letters "k" and "t" in this stanza reflect the precision of his work.

5 An expert. He would set the wing
And fit the bright steel-pointed sock.
The sod rolled over without breaking.
At the headrig, with a single pluck

"rolled" and "breaking" continue the nautical imagery of stanza 1. The sods are like rolling waves rather than waves that crash against the shore — the father is so skilled that he can roll the sod smoothly without breaking it.

This use of enjambment imitates how his father turns the horses round to start a new furrow.

Of reins, the sweating team turned round
10 And back into the land. His eye
Narrowed and angled at the ground,
Mapping the furrow exactly.

This stanza change emphasises the contrast between the father's skill and the clumsiness of his son — it's unlikely he'll grow up to be like his father.

The reference to a ship's wake creates an image of choppy water — this emphasises how the son found it difficult to follow his father.

I stumbled in his hob-nailed wake,
Fell sometimes on the polished sod;
15 Sometimes he rode me on his back
Dipping and rising to his plod.

This paternal image shows how the narrator and his father have a good relationship — he's patient and loving with his son.

He describes his father like a ship, riding the "Dipping" and "rising" 'waves' of the furrows. The rhythm of the poem itself seems to dip and rise — this imitates the boy's movement on his father's back.

He felt like a failure for not learning how to plough.

I wanted to grow up and plough,
To close one eye, stiffen my arm.
All I ever did was follow
20 In his broad shadow round the farm.

"plough" and "follow" are only half-rhymes — this lack of a full rhyme emphasises how the son has not fulfilled his desire to follow in his father's footsteps.

He felt like he was living in his father's shadow. He wanted to be as skilful and impressive as he was.

I was a nuisance, tripping, falling,
Yapping always. But today
It is my father who keeps stumbling
Behind me, and will not go away.

The list of verbs and enjambment emphasises the narrator's clumsy persistence.

This emphasises how the 'Follower' in the title is now the father, not the narrator — the title refers to both of them at different times of their lives.

This is ambiguous — the speaker may be frustrated that his father won't go away, or he may be glad that they still have a strong bond.

Caesura makes this change to the present tense sudden and unexpected — this heightens the impact of the final few sentences.

In line 13 the boy was stumbling behind his father. Now the roles are reversed.

POEM DICTIONARY
globed — rounded (like a globe)
shafts — wooden poles which harness the animal to the plough
furrow — a long, narrow trench in the soil made by the plough
wing — part of the frame of the plough
sock — the end of the plough that cuts the soil
sod — grass-covered earth
headrig — the end of the ploughed part of the field where the
    horse has to turn round
team — the horses pulling the plough
hob-nailed — boots with nails hammered through the soles for grip
wake — the path left by a ship as it moves through the water

Seamus Heaney

Seamus Heaney (1939-2013) was born in Northern Ireland and grew up on his father's farm. 'Follower' was published in 1966 in a poetry collection which dealt with themes of childhood, identity and rural life.

You've got to know what the poem's about

1) The narrator describes his father's <u>expert</u> ploughing. As a boy, he greatly <u>admired</u> his father's <u>skill</u>.

2) The boy <u>followed</u> his father around the farm. Sometimes he'd <u>stumble</u> and <u>fall</u>, and occasionally his father would <u>carry</u> him on his back.

3) He wanted to grow up to be <u>like</u> his father, but all he ever did was <u>follow</u> him around being a <u>nuisance</u>.

4) Now they're both <u>older</u>, the relationship has been <u>reversed</u>, and it's the father who 'follows' his son.

Learn about the form, structure and language

1) **FORM** — The poem is made up of <u>six stanzas</u>, each <u>four lines</u> long, and is written mostly in <u>iambic tetrameter</u>. This <u>neat structure</u> and <u>steady rhythm</u> mimics the action of ploughing. There's a regular <u>ABAB</u> rhyme scheme, but some are only <u>half-rhymes</u> — this reflects how the boy <u>falls short</u> of being like his father.

2) **STRUCTURE** — The first three stanzas focus on the <u>father</u>. The next two stanzas focus on the boy's struggle with his <u>identity</u> — he <u>admired</u> his father and wanted to be <u>like</u> him, but <u>failed</u>. There is a <u>role reversal</u> in the last stanza — now the father is "stumbling / Behind" his son.

3) **NAUTICAL IMAGERY** — The narrator uses language of the <u>sea</u> and <u>sailing</u> to describe his father's ploughing. This emphasises the father's <u>strength</u> and <u>skill</u> and the <u>admiration</u> the boy felt for him. The narrator describes his father as the <u>sails</u>, the <u>captain</u> and the <u>ship</u> itself — he's <u>everything</u> to his son.

4) **REFLECTIVE LANGUAGE** — The narrator sees himself as a "<u>nuisance</u>", and maybe a <u>failure</u>, but at the end of the poem he <u>understands</u> that the father he <u>admired</u> so much as a boy is now <u>dependent</u> on him.

Remember the feelings and attitudes in the poem

Geoff dreamed of being a Roman chariot-racer.

1) **ADMIRATION** — The narrator <u>admires</u> his father's skill at ploughing. As a child, he <u>hero-worshipped</u> him and <u>hoped</u> to take his place one day, despite <u>struggling</u> to follow him.

2) **SELF-CRITICISM** — The narrator worries that he's a <u>failure</u> because he didn't follow in his father's footsteps.

3) **FAMILY TIES** — Despite not following in his father's footsteps, the narrator still has a <u>close relationship</u> with him — he "<u>will not go away</u>".

Go a step further and give a personal response

Have a go at <u>answering</u> these <u>questions</u> to help you come up with <u>your own ideas</u> about the poem:

Q1. What impression do you get of the narrator's father from the poem?

Q2. Do you think the narrator is troubled by the fact that he did not grow up to be like his father?

Q3. Do you think the narrator is annoyed that his father "will not go away"?

KEY THEMES

Family relationships, getting older, nature...

Admiration and relationships changing over time also feature in 'Before You Were Mine', strong family bonds in 'Climbing My Grandfather' and 'Mother, Any Distance', and nature in 'Letters From Yorkshire'.

Mother, Any Distance

He addresses her directly. The poem is like a personal message to her.

A "single span" is the distance between his outstretched hands — he needs two people to measure anything larger than this. It's a small distance, which suggests that his mother's support is still important to him.

"doors and floors" rhyme, but "hands" and "span" is only a half-rhyme — this shows the dislocation between him and his mother.

Holding the start of the tape measure could stand for the time when he was born.

Metaphors and hyperbole create images of vast, open spaces — this hints at adventure and exploration, but also suggests that he feels daunted.

Moving away from his mother physically, but also emotionally.

The tape represents their shared history, but enjambment imitates how they're crossing into a new phase of their relationship.

He's a kite starting to fly, but his anchor mother still keeps him secure. These two one-word sentences slow the pace of the poem, suggesting that he feels apprehensive and thoughtful.

Space metaphor reflects how he feels that being on his own is an exciting adventure, but it's also scary. It emphasises that this is a new experience for him.

Their relationship needs to change. He is trying to move away and she's trying to hold on.

The ellipsis could reflect how the tape is being stretched out, or it could suggest that his mother finally lets go of the tape.

Bird imagery suggests hatching and 'flying the nest' — he's breaking free of his mother's protection, but doesn't know if he'll succeed without her security. The two short lines "has to give" and "to fall or fly" emphasise this message.

He feels there's no limit to the opportunities open to him — they can't be measured like the walls. His tone is optimistic, in contrast to the uncertainty of the final line.

The use of the word "pinch" suggests how desperately she doesn't want to let him go. However, it also suggests pain — if she doesn't let him go, she'll hurt him.

Mother, any distance greater than a single span
requires a second pair of hands.
You come to help me measure windows, pelmets, doors,
the acres of the walls, the prairies of the floors.

5 You at the zero-end, me with the spool of tape, recording
length, reporting metres, centimetres back to base, then leaving
up the stairs, the line still feeding out, unreeling
years between us. Anchor. Kite.

I space-walk through the empty bedrooms, climb
10 the ladder to the loft, to breaking point, where something
has to give;
two floors below your fingertips still pinch
the last one-hundredth of an inch ... I reach
towards a hatch that opens on an endless sky
15 to fall or fly.

POEM DICTIONARY
pelmets — boards or material above a window which hide the curtain rail

Simon Armitage

Simon Armitage was born in 1963 in West Yorkshire and studied Geography at university. This poem was published in 1993. As well as poetry, he writes for TV, film and radio and has also written stage plays.

You've got to know what the poem's about

1) The narrator's <u>mother</u> comes to the house he's moving into to help <u>measure</u> things such as walls and doors.

2) She holds the <u>end</u> of the tape measure while he walks away to measure things. This makes him think about how she's always <u>looked after him</u> — but now she has to <u>let him go</u>.

3) The narrator is <u>looking forward</u> to being independent, but he's also a bit <u>scared</u> by it. He doesn't know if he'll <u>succeed</u> without his mum or not, but there are hints that she'll <u>always be there</u> for him if he needs her.

Learn about the form, structure and language

1) **FORM** — This poem is loosely written in the form of a <u>sonnet</u> — sonnets are traditionally used for <u>love</u> poetry, so this choice of form shows that the speaker still <u>loves</u> his mother. Unlike a sonnet, the poem has an <u>irregular</u> rhyme scheme — this reflects the narrator's feeling of <u>uncertainty</u>. The <u>uneven lines</u> of the last stanza reflect how the <u>bond</u> between mother and son is reaching "<u>breaking point</u>".

2) **STRUCTURE** — The speaker talks about how he <u>needs</u> his mother in the first stanza. In the second stanza he begins to explore <u>independence</u>, and in the last stanza he understands that "<u>something / Has to give</u>" if he's going to be <u>independent</u>. The poem ends with the reader <u>unsure</u> whether he will "<u>fall</u>" or "<u>fly</u>".

3) **LANGUAGE ABOUT MEASUREMENT** — Measurements and distances are an <u>extended metaphor</u> in this poem. They represent the poet's changing relationship with his <u>mother</u>.

4) **LANGUAGE ABOUT MOVEMENT** — Movement is used to show how the poet is <u>breaking away</u> from his mother. Walking around his new house is like <u>exploring</u> a new world, and he feels ready to try to "<u>fly</u>".

5) **IMAGERY** — The visual image of the <u>tape</u> as a link between the mother and son suggests an <u>umbilical cord</u> (a cord that connects a baby in the womb to its mother). The image of the narrator as a "<u>Kite</u>" and his mother as an "<u>Anchor</u>" suggests that she keeps him <u>secure</u>. At the end of the poem, this link seems to be about to <u>break</u>, which shows that the narrator is <u>breaking away</u> from his mother.

Remember the feelings and attitudes in the poem

1) **EXCITEMENT** — The narrator is <u>excited</u> about being independent in his new life.

2) **FEAR** — He's also <u>worried</u> by the thought of being on his own.

3) **CONNECTION** — The tape represents the <u>strong bond</u> between mother and son.

4) **APPRECIATION** — He appreciates her <u>help</u> and the <u>security</u> she offers him.

'One small step into my new house, one giant leap onto the property ladder.'

Go a step further and give a personal response

Have a go at <u>answering</u> these <u>questions</u> to help you come up with <u>your own ideas</u> about the poem:

Q1.   What do the words "Anchor. Kite." tell you about the narrator's relationship with his mother?

Q2.   Do you think the narrator's mother lets go of the tape? Why do you think this?

Q3.   What is the effect of the final rhyme?

KEY THEMES

Family relationships, independence, getting older...

'Walking Away' looks at the way that a parent and child's relationship changes over time. You could also compare the presentation of the mother in this poem with that of the mother in 'Before You Were Mine'.

Before You Were Mine

The first three stanzas each start with a reminder of the distance in time between the narrator's birth and her mum's youth and fun.

The present tense is used to talk about an event in the past. This creates a vivid image — she could be imagining it, or looking at a photograph.

Compares her mother with Marilyn Monroe — she was a glamorous and desirable film star, but also a tragic figure who committed suicide aged 36. This could hint at unhappiness to come.

There could be a hint of jealousy here.

Figurative language that suggests energy and exciting possibilities — she may have hoped for a life like a movie heroine.

I'm ten years away from the corner you laugh on
with your pals, Maggie McGeeney and Jean Duff.
The three of you bend from the waist, holding
each other, or your knees, and shriek at the pavement.
5   Your polka-dot dress blows round your legs. Marilyn.

The narrator sees her mother as having freedom before she was born, but she was also restrained by her own mother.

I'm not here yet. The thought of me doesn't occur
in the ballroom with the thousand eyes, the fizzy, movie tomorrows
the right walk home could bring. I knew you would dance
like that. Before you were mine, your Ma stands at the close
10 with a hiding for the late one. You reckon it's worth it.

Her mum wasn't scared of the consequences of enjoying herself.

The narrator was a demanding baby.

This creates a conversational tone.

The decade ahead of my loud, possessive yell was the best one, eh?
I remember my hands in those high-heeled red shoes, relics,
and now your ghost clatters toward me over George Square
till I see you, clear as scent, under the tree,
15 with its lights, and whose small bites on your neck, sweetheart?

Relics are sacred religious objects from the past — to the narrator, her mother's glamour is precious, but "ghost" highlights how it's in the past and won't return.

Simile appeals to the senses to show that her imagination is so vivid that she can smell her mother.

Cha cha cha! You'd teach me the steps on the way home from Mass,
stamping stars from the wrong pavement. Even then
I wanted the bold girl winking in Portobello, somewhere
in Scotland, before I was born. That glamorous love lasts
20 where you sparkle and waltz and laugh before you were mine.

parallelism

The caesura emphasises that the narrator's birth was the turning point in her mum's life.

Sounds like something a parent would say to their child, but here it's the other way around.

Alliteration stresses her mum's defiance and energy.

As a child, the narrator wanted what she couldn't have — her birth meant that her mum couldn't be a "bold girl" any more.

Repetition of "and" emphasises how many energetic qualities the narrator thinks her mother had.

Repeating this emphasises the difference between then and now. It also develops the possessive tone by repeating the word "mine".

Contrasts with "the right walk home" (line 8). Maybe she's made the wrong choice in life.

Autobiographical, but written in controlling, dominant style like a dramatic monologue.
Inversion of natural use of phrase 'before you were mine', possessive pronoun.
movie tomorrow. Romantic, idealised tomorrows
Makes her Mum's fun party-going feel like a lifetime ago

Carol Ann Duffy

Carol Ann Duffy was born in 1955 in Glasgow. In 2009, she became Poet Laureate. This poem, published in 1993, is autobiographical — Duffy is writing about her own personal experiences.

You've got to know what the poem's about

1) The poem seems to begin with the narrator looking at a <u>photograph</u> of her mother having fun with <u>friends</u>. The narrator <u>imagines</u> her mother when she was younger, possibly informed by her mother's own <u>memories</u> and <u>anecdotes</u> — her mother stays out late <u>dancing</u> and isn't put off by being <u>told off</u> by her own mother.

2) The speaker says that her mother was <u>happiest</u> during the ten years before she was born. She remembers <u>glimpses</u> from her childhood of her mum's <u>fun-loving</u> past.

3) She remembers her mum teaching her to <u>dance</u>. She wanted her to be like this more often, but realises that her mum was only really fun-loving and glamorous <u>before</u> she was born.

Learn about the form, structure and language

1) **FORM** — This poem is made up of <u>four equal stanzas</u> of <u>five lines</u>. This <u>consistent</u> form reflects the <u>steady passage</u> of <u>time</u> and the <u>inevitable changes</u> that time brings.

2) **STRUCTURE** — The poem <u>begins</u> and <u>ends</u> with the mother on a <u>pavement</u> — at the beginning she's having <u>fun</u> with her friends and at the end she's walking with her daughter. This <u>emphasises</u> the changes that time has brought — there's a <u>clear division</u> between <u>before</u> and <u>after</u> the poet was born.

3) **EXCITING LANGUAGE** — A lot of the words and phrases used describe how <u>exciting</u>, <u>fun</u> and <u>glamorous</u> the narrator's mum's life was <u>before</u> the narrator was born.

4) **POSSESSIVE LANGUAGE** — The speaker believes that when she was born, she <u>took control</u> of her mum, and took away her <u>freedom</u>. This <u>reverses</u> the typical idea of children wanting to <u>break free</u> from their parents — in this poem, it's the child stopping the parent from having <u>fun</u>.

5) **COLLOQUIAL LANGUAGE** — The speaker uses <u>colloquial</u> language to create an <u>imaginary</u> <u>conversation</u> with her mother — this suggests they have a <u>close</u>, <u>familiar</u> relationship.

Remember the feelings and attitudes in the poem

1) **ADMIRATION** — The narrator <u>admires</u> her mum's <u>glamour</u> and her <u>headstrong</u>, <u>rebellious</u> approach to life.

2) **NOSTALGIA** — She wishes her mum was still <u>fun-loving</u> and <u>carefree</u>. This is <u>ironic</u> — the child wants the version of the mother <u>before</u> the child was <u>born</u>, but this is <u>impossible</u> because then the child <u>wouldn't exist</u>.

3) **SELF-CRITICISM** — The narrator seems to <u>criticise</u> herself for taking away her mum's freedom.

Go a step further and give a personal response

Have a go at <u>answering</u> these <u>questions</u> to help you come up with <u>your own ideas</u> about the poem:

Q1.   What evidence is there to suggest that the mother's life was better before her child was born?

Q2.   Why do you think the speaker creates such vivid images of her mother as a young woman?

Q3.   What is the effect of describing the mother's shoes as "relics"?

Family relationships, memory...

You could compare the admiration of the daughter in this poem with the admiration that the son in 'Follower' has for his father. Childhood memories are important in both 'Follower' and 'Eden Rock'.

Section One — The Poems

Winter Swans

Personification of the weather — the heavy rain may reflect the problems in their relationship.

Enjambment emphasises the pause in the weather, and perhaps in their arguing.

Personification of the earth's desperation links to how their relationship is struggling for life.

Multiple meanings — keeping to the edge of the lake, but also keeping their distance from each other and perhaps avoiding the issue that troubles them.

The clouds had given their all —
two days of rain and then a break
in which we walked,

Suggests what the swans are doing is meaningful for the couple.

Caesura creates a pause which emphasises their silence and separation.

5   the waterlogged earth
gulping for breath at our feet
as we skirted the lake, silent and apart,

Image suggests that the couple are weighed down by problems in their relationship.

until the swans came and stopped us
with a show of tipping in unison.
As if rolling weights down their bodies to their heads

Icebergs have more below the surface of the water than they do above it — the metaphor may suggest that the couple keep things hidden from each other and aren't communicating, or it could imply that their relationship has a strong foundation.

The word "halved" suggests separation, but also that the swans were a whole to begin with — this reflects the couple's relationship.

10   they halved themselves in the dark water,
icebergs of white feather, paused before returning again
like boats righting in rough weather.

This is the first time we hear one of them speak to the other — this voice seems to confirm that they've turned a corner in their relationship.

Simile shows it's been a rough time for their relationship, but things are becoming more stable. The rough weather mirrors the rain in stanza 1.

'They mate for life' you said as they left,
porcelain over the stilling water. I didn't reply
15   but as we moved on through the afternoon light,

Porcelain is beautiful and strong — this metaphor reflects the hope that their love will have these qualities.

This verb represents how the disruption in their relationship is settling down.

slow-stepping in the lake's shingle and sand,
I noticed our hands, that had, somehow,
swum the distance between us

Sibilant sounds throughout this stanza create an impression of softness — this reflects the softening of tension between them.

Suggests dancing — they're moving together and in unison like the swans did.

and folded, one over the other,
20   like a pair of wings settling after flight.

Their hands have crossed the physical distance between them, but also the metaphorical distance — they have come closer together emotionally.

They're no longer two separate things, but part of one whole.

Swan imagery to describe them holding hands — this reflects how they're following the example of the swans.

Full stop emphasises the sense that the trouble in their relationship has been resolved.

POEM DICTIONARY
skirted — walked around or avoided
righting — returning to a normal or upright position

Owen Sheers

Owen Sheers was born in Fiji in 1974, but grew up in South Wales. 'Winter Swans' was published in his 2005 collection, *Skirrid Hill*. 'Skirrid' comes from the Welsh word *Ysgariad*, meaning divorce or separation.

You've got to know what the poem's about

1) A couple walk around a lake after two days of <u>bad weather</u>. They <u>don't talk</u> to each other and they walk <u>apart</u> from each other — their relationship is <u>troubled</u>.

2) They stop at the sight of some <u>swans</u> and watch them as they tip underwater — they eventually <u>right themselves</u> and <u>swim away</u>. The swans' display seems to change the <u>mood</u> between the couple.

3) The couple carry on walking and end up <u>holding hands</u> — they seem to have <u>reconciled</u>.

Learn about the form, structure and language

1) **FORM** — The poem is mostly written in <u>tercets</u> (three-line stanzas), which makes each stanza look <u>unbalanced</u>. The <u>uneven</u> line lengths and <u>lack</u> of rhyme scheme also contribute to a feeling of <u>disjointedness</u> — this reflects the <u>troubled nature</u> of the couple's relationship. However, frequent <u>enjambment</u> emphasises its <u>continuity</u>. The final stanza is a <u>couplet</u>, which shows that they've been <u>reunited</u> as a couple.

2) **STRUCTURE** — The narrator and his partner are <u>separated</u> for the first five stanzas, but they <u>reunite</u> in the final two. The swans provide a <u>turning point</u> at the start of stanza three — they're <u>beautiful</u> and <u>inspirational</u>, in contrast to earlier descriptions of nature as a place of <u>suffering</u>. This reflects how the couple have reached a <u>turning point</u> in their relationship.

3) **NATURAL IMAGERY** — Natural imagery reflects how their relationship <u>struggles</u> and then <u>improves</u>. Swans are a <u>metaphor</u> for their <u>relationship</u> — as they're part of the natural world, they show that love is <u>natural</u>. This <u>influences</u> the couple — they hold hands so <u>naturally</u> that they don't even <u>notice</u> it happening.

4) **CONTRASTS** — Language about <u>disturbance</u> and <u>peace</u>, <u>separation</u> and <u>togetherness</u>, <u>leaving</u> then <u>returning</u> is used to show how a couple are <u>making up</u> after a period of <u>conflict</u> in their relationship.

5) **DIRECT SPEECH** — One small piece of <u>dialogue</u> is used in the poem, which <u>shifts</u> the <u>focus</u> back onto the <u>couple</u>. It also <u>breaks</u> the <u>silence</u> — this shows that there's <u>hope</u> for their relationship.

Remember the feelings and attitudes in the poem

1) **TENSION** — It's clear that something has <u>happened</u> between the narrator and his partner — the earth is "<u>gulping for breath</u>" and they walk "<u>silent and apart</u>".

2) **PEACE** — There's a feeling of <u>peace</u> towards the end of the poem. The couple have had their <u>problems</u>, but they <u>return</u> to each other and are <u>settled</u> in the end.

"Stop following me, I've said we're over."

Go a step further and give a personal response

Have a go at <u>answering</u> these <u>questions</u> to help you come up with <u>your own ideas</u> about the poem:

Q1.   Why do you think the poem is set in winter?
Q2.   Why do you think the poet chose to use swans as the metaphor in this poem?
Q3.   What evidence is there that the couple have overcome their problems by the end of the poem?

KEY THEMES

Distance, fulfilment, nature...

Compare the physical and emotional distance here with the distance between the narrator and her lover in 'Sonnet 29'. 'Singh Song!' explores fulfilling relationships, and nature is key to 'Letters From Yorkshire'.

Singh Song!

I run just one ov my daddy's shops
from 9 o'clock to 9 o'clock
and he vunt me not to hav a break
but ven nobody in, I do di lock —

5 cos up di stairs is my newly bride
vee share in chapatti
vee share in di chutney
after vee hav made luv
like vee rowing through Putney —

10 Ven I return vid my pinnie untied
di shoppers always point and cry:
Hey Singh, ver yoo bin?
Yor lemons are limes
yor bananas are plantain,
15 *dis dirty little floor need a little bit of mop*
in di worst Indian shop
on di whole Indian road —

Above my head high heel tap di ground
as my vife on di web is playing wid di mouse
20 ven she netting two cat on her Sikh lover site
she book dem for di meat at di cheese ov her price —

my bride
    she effing at my mum
    in all di colours of Punjabi
25 den stumble like a drunk
    making fun at my daddy

my bride
    tiny eyes ov a gun
    and di tummy ov a teddy

30 my bride
    she hav a red crew cut
    and she wear a Tartan sari
    a donkey jacket and some pumps
    on di squeak ov di girls dat are pinching my sweeties —

35 Ven I return from di tickle ov my bride
di shoppers always point and cry:
Hey Singh, ver yoo bin?
Di milk is out ov date
and di bread is alvays stale,
40 *di tings yoo hav on offer yoo hav never got in stock*
in di worst Indian shop
on di whole Indian road —

Late in di midnight hour
ven yoo shoppers are wrap up quiet
45 ven di precinct is concrete-cool
vee cum down whispering stairs
and sit on my silver stool,
from behind di chocolate bars
vee stare past di half-price window signs
50 at di beaches ov di UK in di brightey moon —

from di stool each night she say,
    How much do yoo charge for dat moon baby?

from di stool each night I say,
    Is half di cost ov yoo baby,

55 from di stool each night she say,
    How much does dat come to baby?

from di stool each night I say,
    Is priceless baby —

POEM DICTIONARY
Singh — a name taken on by all Sikh men
chapatti — an Indian flatbread
plantain — a kind of banana
sari — an Indian dress made up of a long
    length of material wrapped round the body
donkey jacket — a type of short coat,
    often worn by workmen

Section One — The Poems   © Not to be photocopied

Daljit Nagra

Daljit Nagra was born in 1966 in London. His parents emigrated to Britain from India — the experiences of Indian immigrants in Britain influence Nagra's poetry, which can be seen in 'Singh Song!', published in 2007.

You've got to know what the poem's about

1) The narrator is a <u>British Indian</u>. He talks about his life working in his father's <u>corner shop</u>.

2) He's just got <u>married</u> and keeps sneaking out of the shop to spend time with his <u>new wife</u>. She's Indian too but dresses in <u>British clothes</u> and acts in a <u>modern</u>, <u>Western</u> way.

3) The narrator neglects his shop duties — customers <u>complain</u> that he's bad at running the shop.

4) When the shop's shut, the couple sit and <u>talk</u>. He tells his wife how much <u>she means to him</u>.

Learn about the form, structure and language

1) **FORM** — There's no regular rhyme scheme, but the poet uses some <u>rhymes</u> to create a <u>light-hearted tone</u>. The poem features the <u>voices</u> of the narrator's wife and customers, showing how he fits into the <u>community</u>. It's like a song, with <u>verses</u> and a <u>chorus</u>, which makes it sound <u>lively</u> and <u>rhythmic</u>. There's little <u>punctuation</u> — this makes the poem <u>flow</u> in a way that sounds <u>confident</u> and <u>cheerful</u>.

2) **STRUCTURE** — The poem <u>alternates</u> between descriptions of the narrator's <u>marriage</u> and his customers' <u>complaints</u>. The repeated complaints emphasise how <u>often</u> he neglects his work. At the end of the poem, the pace <u>slows down</u> to reflect the <u>intimate</u> scene, and the couple's <u>similar language</u> emphasises their <u>closeness</u>.

3) **HUMOROUS DESCRIPTIONS** — The narrator uses <u>entertaining images</u> to describe his wife and family. He also mixes <u>humour</u> with <u>romantic</u> descriptions, which adds to the <u>light-hearted</u> feel.

4) **CONTRASTS** — Lots of seemingly <u>contradictory</u> things are brought together in the characters within the poem. The narrator shows that people can <u>embrace</u> elements of <u>different</u> cultures to form their own <u>identity</u>.

5) **PHONETIC INDIAN ENGLISH** — The words in the poem are spelt the way they <u>sound</u> when <u>spoken aloud</u> — this helps to give a <u>strong impression</u> of the characters. The voices in the poem <u>combine</u> Indian and English words and accents, which shows the influence of <u>both cultures</u> on the characters.

Remember the feelings and attitudes in the poem

1) **LOVE** — The narrator is in <u>love</u> and <u>proud</u> of his new bride — he enjoys spending time with her. His wife's <u>online dating agency</u> could emphasise the new generation's <u>modern attitude</u> to love.

2) **REBELLION** — The narrator's wife makes <u>fun</u> of his parents. He seems to find her lack of respect <u>amusing</u>, so her impressions are presented as <u>acceptable</u> and even <u>endearing</u>. The narrator also <u>rebels</u> against his father's <u>strict rules</u> about working hours by sneaking off all the time.

Go a step further and give a personal response

Have a go at <u>answering</u> these <u>questions</u> to help you come up with <u>your own ideas</u> about the poem:

Q1.   Do you think the title of the poem is effective? Explain your answer.
Q2.   What does the poem suggest about modern marriage?
Q3.   What is the narrator's attitude towards balancing his marriage and his work?

Family relationships, fulfilment...

The speaker here has a different attitude towards his parents than the speakers in 'Mother, Any Distance' and 'Follower' have. You could compare the fulfilling romantic relationships in this poem and 'Sonnet 29'.

Climbing My Grandfather

Present tense — the reader feels like they're witnessing the climb happening, which creates a sense of adventure.

He feels confident and comfortable with his grandfather, but there's also an element of risk. This climbing vocabulary shows the reader that the poem is going to be an extended metaphor of an imagined climb up a mountain.

This adds danger and excitement to the child's game.

This suggests that he's run into difficulty and is taking a different approach.

Compares the shoes to the dusty foothills of the mountain. Also language about age.

Detail that a child would notice from playing with his grandfather. It suggests he likes gardening, which hints at a connection with nature — possibly explains why he's described as a mountain.

Metaphor for trying to get to know his grandfather.

Enjambment reflects change of direction.

Use of oxymoron creates a child-like simile — it's simple and contradictory. It creates an affectionate image — the grandfather isn't cold like ice is.

Splintered nails sound ugly, but here they give the climber a good grip. This may reflect treatment of old people generally — people don't always value them, but they have a lot to offer.

Just as a ridge is part of a mountain, the scar is part of the grandfather and is something to be explored.

He's making progress in getting to know him — the scar possibly represents a past that the climber didn't know about.

The grandson is sensitive and understanding — he doesn't linger over what might have been painful past experiences for his grandfather.

Climbing imagery turns into the familiar image of a child sitting on an adult's shoulder.

The grandfather enjoys playing with his grandson.

Possibly a metaphor for taking in the things his grandfather says. Also shows that the narrator feels better for talking to him.

Child-like fascination with simple things.

Double meaning — he's also a pupil because he's learning things about his grandfather.

The grandfather's white hair is compared to snow on a mountain top.

His exhaustion shows that it's been a difficult climb — he's been making the effort to get to know his grandfather.

The child may physically feel his grandfather's heat and heartbeat, but this also hints at the grandfather's steady and warm love for his grandson. The simple, monosyllabic line slows the pace of the poem, imitating the grandfather's heartbeat.

Definite language compared to "trying to get a grip" (line 4) and "discover" (line 10) — this emphasises how the narrator has gained knowledge. The short line and enjambment prepares us for some kind of conclusion.

I decide to do it free, without a rope or net.
First, the old brogues, dusty and cracked;
an easy scramble onto his trousers,
pushing into the weave, trying to get a grip.
5 By the overhanging shirt I change
direction, traverse along his belt
to an earth-stained hand. The nails
are splintered and give good purchase,
the skin of his finger is smooth and thick
10 like warm ice. On his arm I discover
the glassy ridge of a scar, place my feet
gently in the old stitches and move on.
At his still firm shoulder, I rest for a while
in the shade, not looking down,
15 for climbing has its dangers, then pull
myself up the loose skin of his neck
to a smiling mouth to drink among teeth.
Refreshed, I cross the screed cheek,
to stare into his brown eyes, watch a pupil
20 slowly open and close. Then up over
the forehead, the wrinkles well-spaced
and easy, to his thick hair (soft and white
at this altitude), reaching for the summit,
where gasping for breath I can only lie
25 watching clouds and birds circle,
feeling his heat, knowing
the slow pulse of his good heart.

POEM DICTIONARY
brogues — strong leather shoes
traverse — travel across something
purchase — firm foothold
screed — a mountain slope covered with loose stones

Andrew Waterhouse

Andrew Waterhouse (1958-2001) was born in Lincolnshire and was a lecturer at an agricultural college in Northumberland. 'Climbing My Grandfather' was published in his first collection of poetry in 2000.

You've got to know what the poem's about

1) The narrator imagines climbing his grandfather, using the extended metaphor of himself as a climber and his grandfather as a mountain.

2) The narrator may be imagining or remembering himself as a child, playing with his grandfather and observing things about him, or he may be using climbing as a metaphor for getting to know him as an adult.

Learn about the form, structure and language

1) **FORM** — This poem is written in the present tense, following the narrator's journey up the mountain as he's imagining it. Enjambment imitates the motion of climbing and emphasises the climber's steady progress. Visually, the poem looks strong and solid like a mountain.

2) **STRUCTURE** — The poem follows a climber's progress up a mountain from the bottom to the summit — it feels as though he's getting higher with each line of the poem.

3) **LANGUAGE ABOUT MOUNTAINS** — The extended metaphor of the grandfather as a mountain shows how the grandson sees him — as a permanent, reliable part of his life, and something impressive to explore.

4) **LANGUAGE ABOUT EXPLORATION** — The climbing metaphor creates a sense of adventure that reflects the child's excitement and enjoyment at playing with his grandfather. The child-like way in which he notices and describes things shows how he's fascinated by the features he discovers.

5) **LANGUAGE ABOUT PERSONAL DISCOVERY** — The poem can also be read as the words of an adult who is learning about his grandfather — it is adult in tone and uses complex language. The climbing metaphor shows how the narrator is actively trying to get to know his grandfather as a person.

Remember the feelings and attitudes in the poem

1) **INQUISITIVENESS** — The speaker has a simple, child-like curiosity about his grandfather. This interest is reflected in his adventurousness and fascination with small details.

2) **EFFORT** — The narrator wants to make the effort to get to know his grandfather and to be close to him — this is shown in the physical nature of the climb and the exhaustion he feels at the end.

3) **CLOSENESS** — The way the narrator affectionately describes exploring his grandfather, and the way the grandfather smiles, show that they feel comfortable with each other. Their physical closeness as he's climbing reflects their close emotional relationship.

Go a step further and give a personal response

Have a go at answering these questions to help you come up with your own ideas about the poem:

Q1.   What do you learn about the grandfather's character?

Q2.   Why do you think the narrator chose to make his grandfather the subject of this poem?

Q3.   How do you think the narrator feels after completing his 'climb'?

Family relationships, getting older...

Compare the bond between the speaker and his grandfather with the bond between the speaker and his parents in 'Eden Rock'. Take a look at 'Follower' for another poem where child-like love is presented.

Section One — The Poems

Practice Questions

Roses are red, violets are blue, answer these questions and it will help you (to do really well in the exam). Genius. I'm off to email some publishers while you give these questions a go — see you on the other side.

When We Two Parted

1) Briefly explain what the poem is about.

2) What do you think is the main emotion in the poem? Explain your answer.

3) Find a reference to death in the poem. What effect does it have?

Love's Philosophy

1) Give a summary of the speaker's argument in the poem.

2) Describe the narrator's feelings towards the woman he's addressing.

3) Find an example of physical language in the poem and explain its effect.

Porphyria's Lover

1) Briefly explain what happens in the poem.

2) How do the narrator's emotions change over the course of the poem?

3) What is the rhyme scheme of the poem? What effect does this have?

Sonnet 29 — 'I think of thee!'

1) Briefly explain the extended metaphor that is used in the poem.

2) What is the main mood of the poem? Does this mood change at any point?

3) What effect does the use of exclamation marks have?

Neutral Tones

1) What do you think Hardy is saying about the nature of love?

2) How does the narrator convey a sense of lifelessness and pessimism?

3) What does it mean to say that the poem's structure is 'cyclical'? What is the effect of this structure?

Practice Questions

The Farmer's Bride

1) Briefly describe what happens in the poem.

2) How does the poet convey the farmer's increasing sense of frustration?

3) Find two examples of similes in the poem. Describe the effect of each one.

Walking Away

1) What do you think the overall message of the poem is?

2) Find an example of a simile in the poem. What effect does it have?

3) How does the metaphor comparing the son to a "half-fledged thing" show the narrator's feelings?

Letters From Yorkshire

1) Briefly explain what the poem is about.

2) Why do you think communication with the letter writer is so important to the narrator?

3) Find an example of caesura in the poem and explain why it has been used.

Eden Rock

1) Briefly describe the scene that is presented in the poem.

2) How does the narrator emphasise the strength of family bonds in the poem?

3) Why do you think the narrator describes his parents in such vivid detail? What is the effect of this?

Follower

1) Briefly describe what happens in the poem.

2) Explain the narrator's emotions in the first five stanzas.

3) What is the effect of the sudden change to the present tense in the final stanza?

Practice Questions

Mother, Any Distance

1) Briefly describe what you think the poet is saying about parent/child relationships.

2) Based on evidence in the poem, what emotions do you think the narrator's mother is feeling?

3) Why do you think the poem has an irregular rhyme scheme?

Before You Were Mine

1) Briefly explain what the poem is about.

2) Find an example of possessive language in the poem. What does it tell you about the relationship between the narrator and her mother?

3) How is language used to show the closeness between the narrator and her mother?

Winter Swans

1) Briefly summarise what happens in the poem.

2) How does the mood change as the poem progresses?

3) What is the effect of the small piece of direct speech in the poem?

Singh Song!

1) Briefly explain what the poem is about.

2) How would you describe the tone of the poem? Does the tone change at any point?

3) Find a humorous image in the poem. What effect does this have?

Climbing My Grandfather

1) What do you think the poem is about? Explain your answer.

2) How do you think the grandson feels about his grandfather? Explain your answer.

3) What is the effect of the use of enjambment?

Practice Questions

Everyone loves exams, so this page full of exam-style questions is a real treat. If you're one of those strange people who doesn't like exams, give some of these a go anyway — the more time you spend getting your head around these poems, the easier you'll find the real exam. Oh, and don't forget to write a plan before you start.

Exam-style Questions

1) Compare the way poets present ideas about power in relationships in 'Porphyria's Lover' and one other poem from 'Love and Relationships'.

2) Explore the ways in which romantic relationships are portrayed in 'Singh Song!' and one other poem from 'Love and Relationships'.

3) Compare the poets' feelings towards their parents in 'Mother, Any Distance' and one other poem from 'Love and Relationships'.

4) 'Love is stronger than death'.

   Using this statement as a starting point, compare the way that death is presented in 'Eden Rock' and one other poem from 'Love and Relationships'.

   Remember to comment on how the poems are written.

5) 'Time brings no relief from the pain of love.'

   Using this statement as a starting point, compare the way that the loss of love is presented in 'When We Two Parted' and one other poem from 'Love and Relationships'.

   Remember to comment on how the poems are written.

Romantic Love

If, like me, you're bitter and don't only want to read about happy, smug people in love, then you're in luck...

> 1) A lot of poetry is written about romantic love — not surprising
>   as it's one of the most intense feelings we can have.
>
> 2) People have different experiences of romantic love.

Some people long for each other...

Love's Philosophy (Pages 4-5)

1) The narrator longs to be with the woman he's addressing in the poem. The whole poem is a passionate argument designed to persuade her that they should come together in the same way that nature does.

2) He believes that "Nothing in the world is single" and is frustrated that all of nature is in harmony except for him and his lover. This lack of harmony is reflected in the disruption of the regular rhyme scheme by two half-rhymes — "river"/"ever" and "heaven"/"forgiven".

3) The repetition of physical language such as "clasp" and "kiss" emphasises his desire for her.

Sonnet 29 — 'I think of thee!' (Pages 8-9)

1) The narrator can't stop thinking about her lover when they're not together — she compares her thoughts to "wild vines" which cover a tree until there's "nought to see".

2) She isn't satisfied with just thinking about her lover. She calls her thoughts the "straggling green" which "hides" him — she's concerned that her thoughts will obscure the reality of him.

3) In the nineteenth century, a woman was expected to be reserved about her feelings and to submit to her husband's will. Instead, the narrator expresses her desire (e.g. telling her lover to "set thy trunk all bare"), and commands him to "Renew" his presence in her life. The fact that she defies social convention emphasises the strength of her longing.

...but this can be destructive

Porphyria's Lover (Pages 6-7)

1) The cold cottage reflects the narrator's feelings of loneliness and despair when he's not with Porphyria. He listens for her "with heart fit to break" — his longing has pushed him to breaking point.

2) The narrator says that Porphyria is too "weak" to overcome her "pride" and "vainer ties" to be with him. This reveals his frustration — he yearns for her and doesn't seem to like her spending time elsewhere.

3) His desperation to keep Porphyria with him leads him to murder her — his love has become destructive.

The Farmer's Bride (Pages 12-13)

1) The farmer's focus on his bride's physical features, such as her "soft young down", shows that he longs for a physical relationship, but she's afraid of him.

2) In the last stanza, his exclamation "Oh! my God!" and the repetition "the brown, / The brown of her — her eyes, her hair, her hair!" suggest that he's struggling to control his desire for her.

3) This shows his building frustration, and hints that he may resort to force to get what he wants.

Romantic Love

Some people find fulfilment in their relationships...

Sonnet 29 — 'I think of thee!' (Pages 8-9)

1) The narrator feels "<u>deep joy</u>" when she's with her lover, which suggests that their relationship is fulfilling. The "<u>new air</u>" she breathes implies that she feels <u>revived</u> when she's with him.

2) She <u>celebrates</u> her love for him — the use of <u>exclamation marks</u> emphasises her <u>excitement</u>.

Singh Song! (Pages 28-29)

1) The narrator has a <u>happy</u> marriage. He and his wife enjoy spending <u>time</u> together — at <u>night</u>, when the shop is empty, they <u>sit downstairs</u> together and gaze at the moon.

2) He seems to love <u>everything</u> about her, even aspects of her personality which seem <u>unpleasant</u> — he doesn't mind that she <u>swears</u> at his mum, <u>makes fun</u> of his dad and has the "<u>tiny eyes ov a gun</u>".

3) The couple are <u>romantic</u> and <u>affectionate</u> — they sit together at night, and they call each other "<u>baby</u>". The <u>phonetic</u> spelling of their shared accent (e.g. "dat" and "di") emphasises their <u>closeness</u>.

Winter Swans (Pages 26-27)

1) Although the couple are initially going through a <u>tough</u> time in their relationship, they <u>overcome</u> their difficulties, mirroring the swans who return to the water's surface "<u>like boats righting in rough weather</u>".

2) The use of <u>direct speech</u> signals a <u>turning point</u> — the statement that swans "<u>mate for life</u>" shows the couple's <u>realisation</u> that their own relationship is <u>permanent</u> and can <u>survive</u> difficult times.

3) The simile comparing the couple's hands to "<u>a pair of wings settling after flight</u>" shows that they have reconnected physically and emotionally. The word "<u>settling</u>" creates a feeling of <u>comfort</u> and <u>peace</u>.

...while others experience loss

When We Two Parted (Pages 2-3)

1) The narrator is <u>badly affected</u> by the loss of his lover. <u>Funeral</u> references (e.g. the death "<u>knell</u>") suggest that the narrator <u>grieves</u> for their relationship as though his lover has <u>died</u>.

2) He says that her "<u>vows are all broken</u>" — she's broken the <u>promises</u> she made to him. This suggests he's lost more than just his lover — he's lost the <u>trust</u> he had in her as well.

3) His loss is <u>intensified</u> by the fact that their affair was "<u>secret</u>", so he can't even <u>talk</u> about his pain.

Neutral Tones (Pages 10-11)

1) Whenever the narrator is <u>hurt</u> by love, he <u>remembers</u> the day his relationship broke down. This day made him believe that all "love <u>deceives</u>" — he didn't just lose his lover, but also his <u>faith</u> in love.

2) The landscape is <u>drained</u> of colour — the leaves are "<u>grey</u>" and the sun is "<u>white</u>". The <u>lifeless</u> landscape mirrors the <u>death</u> of the relationship and the narrator's sense of <u>loss</u>.

Other poems also feature longing, fulfilment and loss...

Relationships with family or friends can feature the same feelings as romantic relationships. 'Climbing My Grandfather' is about a fulfilling relationship, whilst 'Walking Away' and 'Before You Were Mine' feature loss.

Family Relationships

On to a different sort of love now, but still lots of emotions flying around. No creepy murderers though. Phew.

> 1) Relationships between parents and children <u>change</u> as children <u>grow up</u>.
>
> 2) There's sometimes <u>tension</u> in family relationships, but also <u>closeness</u> and <u>love</u>.

Some poems explore children becoming independent...

Walking Away (Pages 14-15)

1) The boy walking away from his father towards school represents his first steps towards <u>independence</u>.

2) <u>Negative imagery</u> shows the father's <u>distress</u> at watching his son take his first <u>uncertain</u> steps away from his <u>protection</u> — he compares him to a "<u>satellite / Wrenched from its orbit</u>" and a "<u>half-fledged</u>" bird to show how he sees his son as <u>helpless</u> and <u>vulnerable</u>.

3) However, the <u>reflective tone</u> of the final two lines shows that the father now <u>accepts</u> that "letting go" of children is <u>necessary</u> if they're to become <u>independent</u>.

Mother, Any Distance (Pages 22-23)

1) The narrator <u>addresses</u> his mother <u>directly</u> as she helps him to measure his new house, emphasising her <u>importance</u> in his life. The tape measure that they're holding represents their <u>bond</u>, and the narrator walking away whilst holding the tape symbolises his search for <u>independence</u>.

2) The narrator has <u>mixed feelings</u> about becoming independent. He compares walking round the house to a "<u>space-walk</u>". He's exploring new territory — this is <u>exciting</u>, but also <u>daunting</u>.

3) His mother's fingers "<u>pinch</u>" the tape as it reaches "<u>breaking point</u>" — she's <u>reluctant</u> to let him go, but mother and son need to <u>redefine</u> their relationship, so that he can become <u>independent</u>.

...but others emphasise the strong bond between family members

Climbing My Grandfather (Pages 30-31)

1) The image of a child <u>physically</u> climbing his grandfather implies <u>closeness</u> — the child's <u>trust</u> is shown by him climbing "<u>without a rope or net</u>". The grandfather's <u>patience</u> as his grandson climbs shows his <u>attachment</u> to the child, and his "<u>smiling mouth</u>" indicates <u>enjoyment</u> at spending time with him.

2) The poem could also be read as an <u>adult</u> narrator's effort to get to <u>know</u> his grandfather. The physical <u>exertion</u> of climbing shows the <u>effort</u> the narrator puts into learning about him. Their <u>physical proximity</u> reflects their growing <u>emotional closeness</u> as he finds out more about his grandfather.

Eden Rock (Pages 18-19)

1) The narrator imagines that his parents are "<u>waiting</u>" for him and <u>won't move on</u> until he <u>joins</u> them. This shows the <u>strength</u> of the <u>bond</u> between parents and children.

2) The scene the narrator describes is <u>peaceful</u> and <u>idyllic</u>. The <u>beautiful</u> descriptions of his mother (e.g. "<u>Her hair... takes on the light</u>") and specific everyday <u>details</u> (e.g. "<u>tin cups painted blue</u>") show how <u>fondly</u> he remembers spending time with his parents.

3) It's possible that the narrator is talking about <u>crossing into death</u> — he seems <u>reassured</u> by his parents' promise that "Crossing is <u>not as hard</u> as you might think", suggesting that even death holds <u>less fear</u> if they are there.

Family Relationships

Some people look up to their parents...

Follower (Pages 20-21)

1) Nautical imagery shows the narrator's admiration for his father's strength and skill at ploughing. He compares his father to both the ship and the captain — his powerful shoulders are like a "full sail" and he's "Mapping the furrow exactly", like a captain accurately navigating the sea.

2) As a child, the narrator followed his father, but he "stumbled" and "fell". His literal struggle to follow his father symbolises his struggle to be like him.

3) The half-rhymes in the poem, e.g. "plough" and "follow", emphasise the narrator's sense of failure — he was unable to live up to his father's example.

Before You Were Mine (Pages 24-25)

1) The narrator admires her mother's beauty as a young woman — she highlights it by comparing her to "Marilyn" (Monroe) and by referring to a "thousand eyes", which suggests that she was the centre of attention.

2) She also respects her rebellious nature — the short sentence, "You reckon it's worth it." suggests that the narrator's mother valued fun over rules or pleasing her own mother. The narrator wants to know this "bold girl".

3) Appeals to the senses (e.g. "shriek", "laugh" and "clear as scent") create a vivid picture of the young woman the narrator imagines. This emphasises her vibrancy and the appeal this holds for the narrator.

4) The narrator's admiration is tinged with regret — she tries to recreate her mother's youth from objects such as her "high-heeled red shoes", and seemingly from photos and anecdotes, but it's impossible for her to know her mother before she was born.

I had a look through some photos of my mother from before I was born. Disappointing.

...whereas others rebel against them

Singh Song! (Pages 28-29)

1) The narrator runs one of his "daddy's shops", which suggests that he's dependent on his father. However, he rebels against his father's strict attitude to work — although his father tells him "not to hav a break", he locks the door when the shop is empty and sneaks upstairs to see his wife.

2) The narrator's wife swears at his mother "in all di colours of Punjabi" and makes fun of his father. The narrator describes her behaviour in a light-hearted, humorous way, which shows that he doesn't mind her being disrespectful towards his parents.

3) Respect for elders is an important part of traditional Indian culture — the narrator and his wife are rebelling against their Indian heritage as well as against his parents.

4) The narrator's respect for and loyalty towards his wife seem to have replaced that for his parents. His preoccupation with her is emphasised by the repetition of "my bride".

OTHER POEMS

'Letters From Yorkshire' also features a strong bond...

In 'Letters from Yorkshire', the nature of the relationship between the narrator and the man who writes to her isn't clear. However, they have a strong bond, similar to a family relationship.

Distance

One judge and a restraining order later, I have plenty of experience of being distant from the one I love...

> 1) Relationships can involve <u>physical</u> and <u>emotional separation</u> from the person you love.
>
> 2) This can be <u>painful</u>, but if the relationship is <u>strong</u> enough, the distance can be <u>overcome</u>.

Distance can be emotional, physical or both

Winter Swans (Pages 26-27)

1) Although the couple are together, there's <u>no physical contact</u> or <u>communication</u> — they walk "<u>silent and apart</u>". This reflects the <u>emotional distance</u> between them.

2) The <u>environment</u> reflects their troubled relationship — the clouds have "<u>given their all</u>", hinting that the couple have been arguing, while the "<u>two days of rain</u>" mirror their <u>unhappiness</u>.

3) The couple's <u>division</u> is echoed by the swans, which are described as being "<u>halved</u>" in the water — "<u>halved</u>" is suggestive of something which was once <u>whole</u> but is now <u>divided</u>.

Walking Away (Pages 14-15)

1) The <u>physical distance</u> between the father and son increases as the son <u>walks away</u>. This marks the <u>end</u> of the son's <u>infancy</u> and total <u>reliance</u> on his parents.

2) The father initially sees this distance as full of <u>danger</u> — he compares it to a pathless "<u>wilderness</u>". This reflects how <u>powerless</u> he feels to <u>protect</u> his son as he starts to find his own way in the world.

3) The father gradually starts to see the distance more <u>positively</u>. He recognises that "<u>selfhood begins with a walking away</u>" — by allowing this distance to form, he enables his son to <u>grow</u> and <u>develop</u>.

Distance can be overcome

Letters From Yorkshire (Pages 16-17)

1) The narrator emphasises the <u>physical distance</u> between herself and the letter writer by describing the "<u>icy miles</u>" between them.

2) However, their "<u>souls tap out messages</u>" to each other — communication allows them to bridge the distance and maintain a <u>deep connection</u>.

3) Their <u>communication</u> enables them to share small <u>everyday details</u>, like the fact that they're "<u>watching the same news</u>" — writing to each other almost allows them to feel like they're <u>together</u>.

Sonnet 29 — 'I think of thee!' (Pages 8-9)

1) The narrator and her lover are <u>separated physically</u>. She describes her thoughts about him as "vines" which "twine and bud" <u>around</u> him. This reflects the <u>physical closeness</u> that she wants.

2) She takes "<u>joy</u>" in the thought of <u>overcoming</u> this distance and her thoughts being "<u>burst, shattered, everywhere!</u>" Her <u>confidence</u> that the distance will be overcome is emphasised by the <u>present tense</u> in the <u>last line</u> of the poem — she imagines it so <u>clearly</u> that it's as if she's actually <u>with</u> him.

Other poems also explore the theme of distance...

The narrator of 'Porphyria's Lover' murders Porphyria to stop her ever being apart from him again. In 'When We Two Parted', the narrator is emotionally and physically distant from his former lover.

Desire and Longing

I'm consumed by desire and longing... the crunchy biscuit base... the creamy filling... ohhh sweet cheesecake.

> 1) In romantic relationships, people can feel desire so <u>strongly</u> that they <u>struggle</u> to deal with it.
>
> 2) Longing isn't just felt in romantic relationships — relationships with <u>friends</u> and <u>family</u> can also provoke this emotion.

Desire for another person can be overwhelming

Porphyria's Lover (Pages 6-7)

1) The narrator's desire for Porphyria is shown through his physical descriptions of her "<u>yellow hair</u>" and "<u>smooth white shoulder</u>". The <u>repetition</u> of "<u>And</u>" in lines 17-20 creates a <u>trance-like</u> effect, which reflects how he's <u>transfixed</u> by her.

2) However, he doesn't just want Porphyria — he wants to <u>possess</u> her. This is emphasised by the <u>repetition</u> of "<u>mine, mine</u>". By killing her, he's able to possess her <u>entirely</u>.

Sonnet 29 — 'I think of thee!' (Pages 8-9)

1) The narrator's thoughts are compared to "<u>wild vines</u>" — this image of <u>rapid</u>, <u>unrestrained</u> growth suggests that her thoughts are <u>out of control</u>.

2) There are hints that such an intense desire can be <u>dangerous</u> — the vines that "<u>insphere</u>" the tree threaten to <u>strangle</u> it. <u>Violent</u> language such as "<u>burst, shattered</u>" also hints that passion can become <u>destructive</u>.

3) When the narrator is in her lover's presence, she feels that she can "<u>breathe... a new air</u>" — this suggests that her desire for him is so <u>strong</u> that she feels he's <u>necessary for life</u>.

Some people long for a different life

Letters From Yorkshire (Pages 16-17)

1) The narrator <u>compares</u> her life to the letter writer's life, asking whether his is "<u>more real</u>". She seems to envy the <u>simplicity</u> of his life and his connection with <u>nature</u>.

2) She describes him "<u>breaking ice on a waterbutt</u>", whereas she is "<u>feeding words onto a blank screen</u>" — his physical work is <u>necessary</u> for day-to-day life, whereas her <u>inactive</u> job isn't. As a result, she worries that her way of life is <u>inferior</u>.

3) The <u>alliteration</u> and <u>assonance</u> in "<u>word</u> of that other <u>world</u>" hints at her <u>regret</u> that the "<u>other world</u>" is so <u>distant</u>, and at her <u>yearning</u> to be part of it.

"I wish I was inside writing dreamy poetry... *sigh*"

Follower (Pages 20-21)

1) As a child, the narrator longs to "<u>grow up and plough</u>" like his father, despite "<u>falling</u>" and "<u>tripping</u>". This shows his <u>determination</u> to follow in his father's footsteps.

2) The description of his father's "<u>broad shadow</u>" shows what an <u>imposing</u> presence he was during the narrator's childhood. It also implies that the narrator's childhood <u>admiration</u> for his father will affect him for the <u>rest of his life</u>.

OTHER POEMS

Feelings of desire and longing are present in other poems...

By the end of 'The Farmer's Bride', it's clear that the narrator is becoming overwhelmed by frustrated desire for his unwilling wife. The narrator of 'Love's Philosophy' also longs to be united with the woman he loves.

Getting Older

Getting older is great. I used to have to study poems, but now I get to write about studying poems. Hang on...

> 1) Relationships <u>change</u> over <u>time</u>.
> 2) As children <u>grow up</u>, their relationship with their <u>parents</u> becomes more <u>complicated</u>.

Children's love is often simple and unquestioning...

Climbing My Grandfather (Pages 30-31)

1) The <u>extended metaphor</u> comparing the grandfather to a mountain shows that the child sees his grandfather as something <u>exciting</u> to <u>explore</u>. The way he watches a pupil "<u>slowly open and close</u>" shows a child-like <u>fascination</u> and <u>curiosity</u>.

2) The mountain metaphor also suggests that the grandfather seems <u>solid</u> and <u>unchanging</u> to the child — this suggests the <u>constant</u>, <u>enduring</u> nature of their relationship.

3) The narrator mentions details that might seem <u>unpleasant</u>, but which <u>interest</u> him, such as the "<u>splintered</u>" fingernails and "<u>old stitches</u>" — this shows that he only sees <u>good</u> in his grandfather.

Follower (Pages 20-21)

1) As a child, the narrator <u>idolises</u> his father — the <u>nautical imagery</u> comparing him to a <u>ship</u> and its <u>captain</u> shows that the father is <u>everything</u> to his son.

2) The way he follows his father around, "<u>Yapping always</u>", shows how much he enjoys <u>spending time</u> with his father and wants to <u>connect</u> with him.

...but relationships become more complex as children grow up

Before You Were Mine (Pages 24-25)

1) As the narrator grows up, she comes to <u>understand</u> that her mother is no longer the "<u>bold girl</u>" she used to be — while they have a <u>close bond</u>, the narrator still <u>longs</u> to know the girl her mother was.

2) She realises that she's <u>responsible</u> for the change in her mother — by becoming a parent, her mother has lost her <u>freedom</u>. As a result, the narrator's <u>love</u> for her mother is mixed with <u>guilt</u>.

3) The <u>question</u> in line 15 suggests a <u>reversal</u> of the usual mother-daughter relationship. It hints at the daughter's <u>possessiveness</u> — she seems <u>jealous</u> of those who knew her mother as a young woman.

Mother, Any Distance (Pages 22-23)

1) The narrator and his mother have a <u>close</u> relationship. When she <u>helps</u> him measure things in his new house, he reports the measurements "<u>back to base</u>" — this shows that she's <u>central</u> to his life.

2) However, he realises that "<u>something / Has to give</u>" in their relationship if he's to live an <u>independent</u> life.

3) The narrator's mother is <u>desperate</u> not to let him go — she continues to hold the tape to "<u>the last one-hundredth of an inch</u>". This suggests how <u>painful</u> it is for a parent to watch a child grow up.

'Walking Away' is also about getting older...

The father in 'Walking Away' realises that his role in his son's life has to change as his son grows up. As he becomes more independent, his life no longer revolves around his father like a "satellite" orbiting a planet.

Death

A page about death following a page about getting older. A tad depressing, but excellent page planning.

> 1) Some poems suggest that love <u>carries on</u> after death.
> 2) Death can <u>symbolise</u> the <u>end</u> of a relationship.

Love can endure beyond death

Porphyria's Lover (Pages 6-7)

1) The narrator wants to <u>preserve</u> the "<u>moment</u>" when he feels Porphyria's love for him is "<u>Perfectly pure</u>" — he believes he can only do this by <u>killing</u> her.

2) He seems to love her <u>more</u> once she's <u>dead</u>. In life, he won't even <u>speak</u> to her, but after he kills her, he plants a "<u>burning kiss</u>" on her cheek and holds her "<u>all night long</u>".

3) He believes that she loves him <u>more</u> in death than in life — when alive, her "<u>pride</u>" and "<u>vainer ties</u>" stop her from being with him, but in death he believes it's her "<u>one wish</u>" to be with him forever.

Eden Rock (Pages 18-19)

1) The narrator believes his parents are "<u>waiting</u>" for him, possibly in the <u>afterlife</u>. The sky "<u>lit by three suns</u>" hints at a <u>heavenly</u> setting, in which the family can be <u>reunited</u> by death.

2) The narrator's parents "<u>beckon</u>" and "<u>call</u>" to him — this shows their <u>eagerness</u> to be with him and demonstrates that their family bond remains <u>strong</u>.

3) The scene is <u>familiar</u> to the narrator — he describes the "<u>same suit</u>" and "<u>same three plates</u>". Even though the family has been <u>separated</u> by the parents' deaths, nothing has changed — this suggests that they're still as <u>close</u> as they were when he was a <u>child</u>.

The end of a relationship can be compared to death

When We Two Parted (Pages 2-3)

1) The narrator's description of his former lover as "<u>Pale</u>" and "<u>cold</u>" makes her sound like a <u>corpse</u>.

2) Hearing her name in connection with <u>other men</u> is like a "<u>knell</u>" (the ringing of a bell to mark a death).

3) The end of their relationship has <u>affected</u> him like a death — his long-lasting "<u>Sorrow</u>" suggests that he's <u>grieving</u> for her, while his "<u>silence and tears</u>" are suggestive of behaviour at a <u>funeral</u>.

Neutral Tones (Pages 10-11)

1) Hardy uses language to do with <u>death</u> to show the <u>loss of love</u> between the narrator and his lover. The narrator describes his lover's "<u>smile</u>" as "<u>the deadest thing / Alive</u>" — this <u>oxymoron</u> emphasises her complete <u>lack</u> of feeling for him.

2) The <u>lifeless</u> and <u>decaying</u> winter landscape reflects the death of their love — the leaves are "<u>grey</u>" and even the sun is cold and "<u>white</u>", offering no warmth or vitality. The "<u>starving sod</u>" lacks the <u>nourishment</u> needed for life — this hints that their relationship didn't have <u>enough love</u> to keep it <u>alive</u>.

Other poems also use images of death...

In 'Winter Swans', the personification of the earth "gulping for breath" suggests that their relationship is dying. The imagery of winter approaching in 'The Farmer's Bride' hints at the death of hope for the couple.

Memory

You might look back fondly on your time spent studying poetry, or it might haunt you for the rest of your days.

> 1) Memories can <u>stay</u> with people for a <u>long time</u>.
> 2) People have <u>vivid</u> memories of times or events which had a <u>big impact</u> on them.

Painful memories never go away

Walking Away (Pages 14-15)

1) The narrator watched his son walk away from him towards school "<u>eighteen years ago, almost to the day</u>". The narrator still remembers the <u>exact day</u> and <u>details</u> such as the "<u>touch-lines new-ruled</u>" — this shows the lasting <u>impact</u> the experience had on him.

2) Language about <u>pain</u> shows how <u>difficult</u> the parting was for the narrator. He says his son was "<u>Wrenched</u>" from him — he feels as though they were <u>forcibly</u> parted.

3) The memory <u>continues</u> to <u>hurt</u> him in the present day — it "<u>Gnaws</u>" at his mind.

Neutral Tones (Pages 10-11)

1) The narrator vividly remembers the <u>end</u> of his relationship and the <u>setting</u> in which it happened — he describes the <u>expression</u> on his lover's face and the pond "<u>edged with greyish leaves</u>."

2) This memory <u>returns</u> to him whenever he has another experience of love going "<u>wrong</u>" — for him, the memory has become a <u>symbol</u> of <u>failed love</u>.

3) The memory is <u>bitter</u> and <u>pessimistic</u>. Even the sun, usually a symbol of warmth and light, is "<u>God-curst</u>" — this hints that the narrator feels his life has been <u>cursed</u> by the memory of the break-up.

Memories can be described vividly

Eden Rock (Pages 18-19)

1) The <u>happy memory</u> of a picnic with his parents <u>occupies</u> the narrator's mind — this shows how <u>important</u> it is to him.

2) The memory is described vividly — the ordinary details of "<u>paper for a cork</u>" and "<u>an old H.P Sauce bottle</u>" paint a <u>rich</u>, <u>lifelike</u> picture.

3) The memory is infused with "<u>light</u>" — this makes the scene seem <u>bright</u> and <u>warm</u>. His mother's hair is the colour of "<u>wheat</u>" and it "<u>takes on the light</u>" — this creates a <u>golden</u>, <u>summery</u> feel.

Gordon had vivid memories of that pond weed he saw three seconds ago...

Follower (Pages 20-21)

1) The first four stanzas describe the narrator's memory of his father ploughing. He uses <u>imagery</u> such as "His shoulders <u>globed like a full sail strung</u>", and <u>onomatopoeia</u>, e.g. "<u>clicking</u> tongue", to paint a <u>powerful</u> picture of his father — this emphasises how <u>carefully</u> he watched him work.

2) The narrator <u>vividly</u> describes the "<u>bright steel-pointed sock</u>" of the plough and the "<u>sod</u>" that "<u>rolled over</u>". The inclusion of such <u>details</u> suggests that these memories are still <u>clear</u> in the narrator's mind, showing how <u>important</u> they are to him.

Think about the theme of memory in other poems...

The narrator in 'When We Two Parted' is still hurt by the memory of a lover. In 'Before You Were Mine', the narrator contrasts her memories of her mother with what she imagines she was like as a young woman.

Nature

The sky outside is a dull, dreary grey. Not a reflection of my mood, just what the weather's like. Again.

1) <u>Positive</u> natural imagery suggests that love is <u>beautiful</u> and <u>natural</u>.
2) <u>Negative</u> natural imagery can be used to show the <u>loss</u> of love.

Natural images are used to symbolise love...

Love's Philosophy (Pages 4-5)

1) The narrator uses natural imagery to <u>argue</u> that "<u>Nothing in the world is single</u>". He believes that he and his lover should follow nature's <u>example</u> — they should be <u>together</u> in the same way that different parts of nature "<u>mingle</u>" and "<u>mix</u>".

2) He <u>personifies</u> nature, claiming that "the mountains <u>kiss</u> high heaven" and "the waves <u>clasp</u> one another". This emphasises his argument that humans are <u>part</u> of the natural world and should behave in the <u>same way</u> as natural entities.

Winter Swans (Pages 26-27)

1) The swans symbolise the couple — the way they "<u>halved themselves</u>" in the water reflects the couple's <u>disconnection</u>. However, the swans then return to the surface "<u>like boats righting in rough weather</u>" — this suggests that the couple's relationship will <u>recover</u>.

2) The couple are <u>positively influenced</u> by nature. At the end of the poem, their hands join "<u>like a pair of wings settling after flight</u>" — they're <u>following</u> the <u>example</u> of the swans.

...but they can also reflect troubled relationships

The Farmer's Bride (Pages 12-13)

1) When the bride married the farmer, she became <u>afraid</u> of "<u>all things human</u>" — the way she's described as being <u>part of nature</u> throughout the poem shows how she has <u>withdrawn</u> from the human world.

2) Her connection with nature <u>attracts</u> the narrator, shown by his description of her as "<u>slight as a young larch tree</u>". However, this connection also creates <u>distance</u> between them and is a source of <u>frustration</u> for the farmer — she talks to the animals, but he says "<u>I've hardly heard her speak at all.</u>"

3) She's frequently compared to small <u>prey</u> animals — "like a <u>hare</u>", "Shy as a <u>leveret</u>". The farmer "<u>chased her</u>" and "<u>caught her</u>", which suggests that he's a <u>predator</u> — this hints at a <u>dangerous</u> relationship.

Neutral Tones (Pages 10-11)

1) Descriptions of a landscape <u>drained</u> of <u>life</u> and <u>colour</u> reflect how the <u>love</u> has drained from the couple's relationship — the sun is "<u>white</u>" and the leaves are "<u>grey</u>".

2) The narrator compares his lover's smile to an "<u>ominous bird a-wing</u>". This could suggest that her smile is like a <u>carrion bird</u> — a bird that feeds on dead animals. This <u>predicts</u> the <u>death</u> of their relationship.

Other poems also feature the theme of nature...

The narrator of 'Sonnet 29' uses vines to symbolise her thoughts about her lover. 'Letters From Yorkshire' and 'Follower' are both about people whose lives are intimately connected with the natural world.

Practice Questions

Everyone feels 'desire and longing' to answer practice questions — they're a great way to test your 'memory' of what you've just read (see what I did there). You don't have to write a whole essay to answer these questions (but you're welcome to try if you've got nothing better to do)* — one or two short paragraphs is fine.

Romantic Love

1) How is the narrator's frustration at not being with his lover conveyed in 'Love's Philosophy'?

2) How does Barrett Browning use language to show feelings of longing in 'Sonnet 29 — I think of thee!'?

3) In 'Porphyria's Lover', how does Browning present the narrator's feelings towards Porphyria as destructive?

4) How does the poet create a sense that things won't end well for the couple in 'The Farmer's Bride'?

5) How does Nagra convey the closeness between the couple in 'Singh Song!'?

6) In 'Neutral Tones', how does Hardy use imagery to present the end of the relationship?

Family Relationships

1) In 'Walking Away', how is the parting presented as difficult for: a) the father?   b) the son?

2) How does the narrator feel about becoming independent in 'Mother, Any Distance'? Explain your answer.

3) In 'Climbing My Grandfather', how does the grandfather feel about his grandson? How can you tell?

4) How does the narrator show his admiration for his father in 'Follower'?

5) In 'Before You Were Mine', what are the narrator's feelings towards her mother? Explain your answer.

6) How does the narrator's love for his wife influence his behaviour towards his family in 'Singh Song!'?

Distance

1) In 'Winter Swans', how does Sheers present the emotional and physical distance between the couple at the start of the poem?

2) Which details emphasise the physical distance between the narrator and the letter writer in 'Letters From Yorkshire'?

3) In 'Sonnet 29 — I think of thee!', how does the narrator present her joy at the thought of overcoming the distance between her lover and herself?

*Really, don't.

Practice Questions

Desire and Longing

1) How is the intensity of the narrator's desire for Porphyria shown in 'Porphyria's Lover'?

2) In 'Letters From Yorkshire', how does the narrator view her life in comparison with the letter writer's life?

3) What does the narrator in 'Follower' long for as a child? How is this longing conveyed?

Getting Older

1) In 'Climbing My Grandfather', how is the narrator's love presented as simple and childlike?

2) In 'Before You Were Mine', how does the narrator think her mother's life was changed by parenthood?

3) In 'Mother, Any Distance', how do the mother's feelings about her son gaining independence contrast with his own feelings about it? Explain your answer.

Death

1) How does the narrator of 'Porphyria's Lover' think death will alter his relationship? Explain your answer.

2) In 'Eden Rock', how does Causley imply that love can endure beyond death?

3) Do you think the comparison between death and the end of a relationship is more effective in 'When We Two Parted' or 'Neutral Tones'? Explain your answer.

Memory

1) In 'Walking Away', how does a memory continue to affect the narrator in the present?

2) How does Causley create such a vivid impression of his childhood memory in 'Eden Rock'?

3) In 'Follower', why do you think Heaney includes detailed descriptions of the plough?

Nature

1) Why does the speaker personify nature in 'Love's Philosophy'?

2) What effect do the swans have on the couple in 'Winter Swans'?

3) How does Mew use natural imagery to create a sense of danger in 'The Farmer's Bride'?

Practice Questions

*When it comes to the exam, you'll be asked to compare two poems that share a common theme.
"But how on Earth do I prepare for that?" I hear you cry. Never fear — have a go at the questions below.
The more comparisons and links that you make between poems now, the easier it'll be come exam time.*

Exam-style Questions

1) Compare the way in which desire and longing is presented in 'The Farmer's Bride' and one other poem from 'Love and Relationships'.

2) 'Relationships change as people grow older.'

   Using this quotation as a starting point, write about the theme of getting older in 'Walking Away' and one other poem from 'Love and Relationships'.

3) Compare the way in which feelings of loss are presented in 'Neutral Tones' and one other poem from 'Love and Relationships'.

4) Compare how poets present the role of nature in a relationship in 'Letters From Yorkshire' and one other poem from 'Love and Relationships'.

5) 'The relationship between a parent and a child is the strongest bond in a person's life'.

   Using this quotation as a starting point, explore the way that relationships are presented in 'Follower' and one other poem from 'Love and Relationships'.

   Remember to comment on how the poems are written.

Forms of Poetry

Poets can write poetry using many different forms. Personally, the form of writing I like most is 'revision guide'.

> 1) Some poems use a <u>traditional</u> form, such as a <u>sonnet</u> or <u>dramatic monologue</u>, whereas others don't stick to a set form.
>
> 2) Form can be used to <u>emphasise</u> the <u>message</u> of a poem.

Sonnets are traditionally about love

Sonnet 29 — 'I think of thee!' (Pages 8-9)

1) 'Sonnet 29' <u>loosely</u> follows the <u>Petrarchan form</u> — the <u>first eight</u> lines (the octave) have <u>one rhyme scheme</u> and the <u>final six</u> lines (the sestet) have a <u>different</u> one. This links the poem to a <u>long tradition</u> of love poetry, which makes the narrator's feelings seem more <u>serious</u> and <u>deep-rooted</u>.

2) In a Petrarchan sonnet, the <u>octave</u> presents a <u>problem</u> and the <u>sestet</u> offers a <u>solution</u>. However, in 'Sonnet 29' the solution (that the narrator's lover should "<u>instantly / Renew thy presence</u>") comes <u>early</u>, halfway through line 7. This reflects the narrator's <u>intense desire</u> to see him.

Mother, Any Distance (Pages 22-23)

1) 'Mother, Any Distance' is written <u>loosely</u> in the <u>sonnet form</u> — it consists of <u>two quatrains</u> and a <u>sestet</u> (with an extra half line). The use of the sonnet form hints at the narrator's <u>love</u> for his mother.

2) This poem <u>differs</u> from a traditional sonnet because it has <u>uneven line lengths</u> and <u>no regular rhyme scheme</u>. This makes the narrator's love seem <u>natural</u> and <u>understated</u>.

3) The first stanza is composed of two <u>rhyming couplets</u>, emphasising the <u>closeness</u> between mother and son. The rhyme scheme <u>breaks down</u> in stanzas two and three, reflecting the way he's <u>pulling away</u> from her. However, the <u>final two lines</u> of the poem rhyme — this suggests that their <u>bond</u> will never break.

Dramatic monologues have a single speaker

Porphyria's Lover (Pages 6-7)

1) The narrator <u>controls</u> the poem, because his is the <u>only voice</u> we hear. This means that the reader only has the information the narrator <u>chooses</u> to give.

2) The <u>regular ABABB rhyme scheme</u> reflects his need for <u>control</u>. The last 'B' rhyme creates a <u>stuttering</u> effect that suggests a spilling over of <u>emotion</u> — this reflects the narrator's <u>madness</u>.

3) As it becomes clear the speaker is <u>mad</u>, the reader must <u>question</u> everything he says. The reader has to come to their <u>own conclusion</u> about Porphyria's feelings and the nature of their relationship.

The Farmer's Bride (Pages 12-13)

1) We only hear the farmer's voice — the bride's side of the story <u>isn't told</u>.

2) However, the farmer's narrative gives <u>information</u> which allows the reader to make a <u>judgement</u>. He says "<u>I chose</u> a maid" and acknowledges that she was "<u>Too young maybe</u>" — this suggests that the woman had <u>no say</u> about the marriage and perhaps <u>wasn't ready</u> for it.

3) The reader has to decide where their <u>sympathy</u> lies — with the <u>farmer</u>, the <u>bride</u>, or <u>both</u>.

Some poems don't have a set form...

'Climbing My Grandfather', 'Winter Swans' and 'Letters From Yorkshire' are written in free verse. This means these poems don't have a set rhyme scheme or metre, which makes them sound like natural speech.

Poetic Devices

Poets use lots of fancy techniques in their poems to make them as effective as possible. Here are just a few...

1) You need to be able to <u>identify</u> different techniques used in the poems and make <u>comparisons</u> between them.

2) It's really important that you don't just <u>say</u> what the technique is, but <u>comment</u> on the <u>effect</u> it creates.

Repetition can be used for emphasis

Love's Philosophy (Pages 4-5)

1) The <u>repetition</u> of "<u>kiss</u>" and "<u>clasp</u>" emphasises that everything in nature acts in the <u>same way</u>. This <u>physical language</u> also draws attention to the narrator's <u>frustration</u> that he can't be with his lover.

2) The <u>repetition</u> of "<u>And</u>" in lines 13 and 14 emphasises just how <u>many</u> examples he can give her to prove his point. Positioning the "And" at the <u>start</u> of each line makes it <u>stand out</u>.

3) The <u>structure</u> of the second stanza <u>repeats</u> the first — most of the stanza <u>builds up evidence</u> and the last line poses a <u>rhetorical question</u>. This repetition makes the argument more <u>forceful</u>.

Singh Song! (Pages 28-29)

1) The repetition of "<u>vee share in</u>" emphasises the couple's <u>closeness</u> and suggests that their relationship is <u>equal</u>. The narrator's repeated references to "<u>my bride</u>" show how <u>proud</u> he is that she's his wife.

2) The repeated <u>chorus</u> of the shoppers' complaints shows that the narrator <u>regularly neglects</u> his job in favour of his wife — this emphasises his <u>preoccupation</u> with her.

3) The words "<u>I say</u>" and "<u>she say</u>" are repeated in lines 51-57. This creates a <u>song-like rhythm</u> that highlights the couple's <u>pleasure</u> in each other's company. The repetition of "<u>baby</u>" shows their <u>affection</u>.

Enjambment can affect how a poem flows

Letters From Yorkshire (Pages 16-17)

1) Enjambment is used throughout 'Letters From Yorkshire' to make it flow like <u>natural speech</u> — this gives the impression that the narrator is talking <u>directly</u> to the letter writer.

2) The enjambment of "<u>seasons / turning</u>" mirrors the <u>changing seasons</u>. It <u>slows</u> the <u>pace</u> of the poem to reflect the slow pace of the letter writer's <u>life</u> and emphasises his <u>connection</u> to <u>nature</u>.

3) The enjambed lines "<u>heartful of headlines / feeding words</u>" emphasises the narrator's growing <u>anxiety</u> about her <u>stressful</u> job. This highlights the <u>contrast</u> between her lifestyle and that of the letter writer.

Mother, Any Distance (Pages 22-23)

1) Enjambment gives the poem a <u>natural</u>, <u>flowing</u> rhythm, which mirrors the son's <u>movement</u> around the house. It also emphasises verbs such as "<u>leaving</u>" and "<u>unreeling</u>", which highlight his <u>efforts</u> to <u>break away</u> from his mother and become independent.

2) In the third stanza, the enjambment emphasises the verbs "<u>climb</u>", "<u>pinch</u>" and "<u>reach</u>" — this highlights how <u>difficult</u> the process of gaining independence is for <u>both</u> mother and son.

3) Enjambment draws out lines such as "<u>something / has to give</u>", reflecting the way the narrator is <u>pulling away</u> from his mother.

Poetic Devices

Punctuation can create pauses in a poem

Porphyria's Lover (Pages 6-7)

1) Caesurae and end-stopping make the poem sound fragmented, which reflects the narrator's unstable mind.

2) The first five lines are end-stopped, which creates a sense of him listening for Porphyria's arrival.

3) There are lots of caesurae in lines 32-41, when the narrator decides to murder Porphyria. This creates a halting, erratic rhythm, suggesting that his mental state is particularly disturbed at this point.

Sonnet 29 — 'I think of thee!' (Pages 8-9)

1) The exclamation mark after "I think of thee!" stresses the narrator's excitement at the thought of her lover.

2) In line 7, a caesura is used to mark the turning point (volta) in the poem — the narrator's thoughts about her lover are replaced by commands that he "Renew" his presence.

3) The caesura in the final line of the poem slows the pace, emphasising the narrator's relief and contentment at the thought of being reunited with her lover.

Climbing My Grandfather (Pages 30-31)

1) Waterhouse uses punctuation to mark the narrator's pauses as he climbs.

2) Caesurae after phrases like "earth-stained hand" and "warm ice" suggest that the narrator stops to focus on these parts of his grandfather, emphasising his fascination.

3) The caesurae in lines 21-23 suggest that the climb is becoming more challenging and the narrator has to pause frequently to catch his breath.

This. Climbing. Lark. Is. So. Darn. Exhausting.

Poets appeal to the senses to create vivid images

Before You Were Mine (Pages 24-25)

1) The narrator appeals to the senses to create a vivid picture of her mother as a young woman.

2) She seems able to both smell and hear the "ghost" of her mother, who is as "clear as scent" and "clatters" towards her. These descriptions create a powerful image.

3) She physically tries to get close to her mother's past by putting her hands in her "high-heeled red shoes".

When We Two Parted (Pages 2-3)

1) The narrator describes the "Pale" sight of his lover's cheek and the "cold" touch of her kiss — this vividly communicates how her love for him has died. The touch of the cold "dew" creates a powerful impression of a chilly early morning — the setting reflects the coldness between him and his lover.

2) The death "knell" is a mournful noise, which emphasises his dismay at hearing about her affairs with other men — this funereal sound confirms the death of his faith in her.

OTHER POEMS

You could also write about the use of contrasts...

'Before You Were Mine' shows how different the mother's life was before and after the narrator was born, and 'Winter Swans' contrasts the distance of the couple at the start of the poem with their closeness at the end.

Use of Sound

Poems are often intended to be read aloud, so the sounds that words make are particularly important.

1) Onomatopoeia is an effective way of using <u>sound</u> to add <u>extra impact</u> to a poem.
2) Poets repeat <u>similar sounds</u> to create a particular <u>mood</u> or <u>effect</u>.

Onomatopoeia can emphasise a character's emotions

Before You Were Mine (Pages 24-25)

1) The <u>energy</u> and <u>liveliness</u> of the mother's "<u>fizzy</u> movie tomorrows" suggests that her future held <u>exciting possibilities</u>. This hints at her <u>hopes</u> of a perfect, fairy-tale life.

2) The <u>onomatopoeic verb</u> "<u>stamping</u>" reflects the <u>frustration</u> that the narrator believes her mother feels about her <u>loss</u> of <u>freedom</u> and <u>potential</u>.

3) The "<u>shriek</u>" of the mother as a young woman contrasts with the "<u>yell</u>" of the narrator as a baby. This highlights the shift from the <u>joy</u> and <u>fun</u> of <u>youth</u> to the <u>responsibilities</u> of <u>motherhood</u>.

Sonnet 29 — 'I think of thee!' (Pages 8-9)

1) The <u>onomatopoeic verb</u> "<u>Rustle</u>" creates a <u>gentle</u> sound — this suggests that the narrator feels her lover's presence could <u>easily</u> replace her thoughts of him.

2) The violent words "<u>burst</u>" and "<u>shattered</u>" emphasise her passion. The <u>plosive</u> "<u>b</u>" and "<u>t</u>" sounds suggest the <u>suddenness</u> with which her thoughts would be destroyed.

Repeated sounds can affect a poem's mood

When We Two Parted (Pages 2-3)

1) The <u>consonance</u> of 'k' sounds in "chee<u>k</u> and <u>c</u>old / <u>C</u>older thy <u>k</u>iss" creates a harsh feel — this emphasises the <u>coldness</u> of the narrator's lover and the narrator's anger at how she has <u>treated</u> him.

2) <u>Sibilant</u> 'sh' sounds in "<u>sh</u>are in its <u>sh</u>ame" emphasise the narrator's <u>silence</u> — the affair was <u>secret</u> and even now he <u>can't talk</u> about it.

3) In the third and fourth stanzas, the <u>assonant</u> long 'ee' sounds in words such as "th<u>ee</u>", "d<u>ee</u>ply" and "dec<u>ei</u>ve" <u>draw out</u> each word — this reflects the <u>long-lasting</u> nature of the narrator's <u>pain</u>.

Letters From Yorkshire (Pages 16-17)

1) <u>Sibilant</u> '<u>s</u>' sounds and <u>assonant</u> '<u>ee</u>' sounds in "<u>see</u>ing the <u>sea</u>son<u>s</u>" emphasise the phrase. This highlights the letter writer's <u>connection</u> with nature and the narrator's <u>longing</u> to lead a similar lifestyle.

2) The <u>alliteration</u> in "<u>h</u>eartful of <u>h</u>eadlines" creates a sense of <u>breathlessness</u>, which highlights the narrator's <u>anxiety</u> about her life.

3) <u>Sibilance</u> in "our <u>s</u>oul<u>s</u> tap out me<u>ss</u>age<u>s</u> acro<u>ss</u> the i<u>c</u>y mile<u>s</u>" creates a <u>chain</u> of '<u>s</u>' sounds, which represents the way their messages <u>cross</u> the distance between them, keeping them <u>connected</u>.

Some poems use plosive sounds...

In 'Porphyria's Lover', plosives in "<u>B</u>lushed <u>b</u>right <u>b</u>eneath my <u>b</u>urning <u>k</u>iss" hints at the force behind the narrator's love. The words "<u>b</u>reaking <u>p</u>oint" in 'Mother, Any Distance' suggest the sound of the tape snapping.

Imagery

Imagery is language that creates a picture — it includes similes, metaphors and personification.

> 1) Personification of <u>nature</u> makes it seem <u>human</u>.
> 2) Poets use <u>metaphors</u> and <u>similes</u> to create <u>powerful descriptions</u>.

Personification can create vivid images

Winter Swans (Pages 26-27)

1) The clouds are personified as having "<u>given their all</u>" — this creates a vivid image of heavy rainfall. It also hints that the couple have been <u>arguing</u> and are now drained of emotion.

2) The personified earth is "<u>gulping for breath</u>" — this creates a powerful image of the earth drowning, hinting that the couple's <u>problems</u> threaten to <u>overwhelm</u> them.

Love's Philosophy (Pages 4-5)

1) The narrator uses words such as "<u>mingle</u>" and "<u>disdain'd</u>" to show <u>nature</u> behaving in a <u>human way</u> — this <u>strengthens</u> his argument that nature and humans are supposed to connect in the <u>same way</u>.

2) The <u>sun</u> is <u>powerful</u> and a <u>source of life</u>, but in the poem it "<u>clasps the earth</u>" — this hints that even the most powerful parts of nature <u>need</u> to form <u>bonds</u> with other parts of nature.

Metaphors and similes add power to descriptions

Follower (Pages 20-21)

1) The narrator uses an <u>extended metaphor</u> of his father as a <u>ship</u> — he likens his father's shoulders to a "<u>full sail</u>", and describes how he "stumbled" in his father's "<u>wake</u>". This emphasises his <u>power</u> and <u>skill</u>.

2) Comparing his father to a ship emphasises how <u>small</u> and <u>powerless</u> the narrator felt as a child, and highlights the <u>awe</u> he felt for his father.

Climbing My Grandfather (Pages 30-31)

1) The narrator describes his grandfather using the <u>extended metaphor</u> of a <u>mountain</u>. This shows that he sees his grandfather as <u>permanent</u>, <u>reliable</u> and worthy of <u>exploration</u>.

2) The "climbing" could refer to a child <u>literally climbing</u> a relative, or it could be a metaphor for <u>learning about</u> his grandfather as an <u>adult</u> — both interpretations show the <u>bond</u> between them.

Walking Away (Pages 14-15)

1) The narrator uses the simile of a "<u>satellite</u>" that is "<u>Wrenched from its orbit</u>" to describe his son walking away — this creates a vivid image of an object <u>lost</u> in space, emphasising the father's <u>anxiety</u>.

2) The metaphor of a "<u>scorching</u>" fire creates a powerful impression of the <u>pain</u> of growing up, but the fact that these experiences "<u>fire one's irresolute clay</u>" illustrates the <u>strength</u> acquired as a result.

Other poems use imagery...

Hardy personifies the "starving sod" in 'Neutral Tones' to create an impression of suffering and death. 'Sonnet 29' uses natural imagery, comparing the narrator's thoughts to "wild vines" and her lover to a "tree".

Rhyme and Rhythm

— there's no excuse for spelling 'rhythm' wrong in the exam.

1) Rhyme and rhythm affect the <u>mood</u> of a poem and how it <u>flows</u>.
2) They can also be used to create a particular <u>effect</u> or to emphasise the <u>message</u> of the poem.

Rhyme can add power to the poet's message

Neutral Tones (Pages 10-11)

1) The <u>ABBA</u> rhyme scheme mirrors the <u>cyclical structure</u> of the poem — just as the poem <u>begins</u> and <u>ends</u> with the image of the <u>pond</u>, the <u>'A' rhyme returns</u> at the <u>end</u> of each stanza. This reflects the way that the narrator's <u>memory</u> of the break-up <u>returns</u> to affect him.

2) Most of the rhyming words are <u>monosyllabic</u>, e.g. "<u>day</u>" / "<u>grey</u>" and "<u>God</u>" / "<u>sod</u>". This creates a <u>deadening</u> effect at the end of each line, which <u>emphasises</u> the <u>passionless</u> tone of the poem.

Sonnet 29 — 'I think of thee!' (Pages 8-9)

1) The poem <u>doesn't follow</u> a standard sonnet rhyme scheme. Instead, the '<u>B</u>' rhyme ("<u>tree</u>", "<u>see</u>" etc.) is used <u>throughout</u> the poem — this reflects the narrator's <u>constant</u>, <u>unchanging</u> feelings for her lover.

2) The word "<u>thee</u>" is used as an end-rhyme <u>four times</u> — this emphasises her <u>obsession</u> with him.

A poem's rhythm affects its pace and mood

When We Two Parted (Pages 2-3)

1) The mostly <u>consistent metre</u> and <u>strong rhyme scheme</u> gives the poem a <u>regular rhythm</u>. This drives the poem <u>forward</u> and gives a sense of <u>certainty</u>, reflecting the narrator's <u>conviction</u> of his long-lasting pain.

2) Most lines have <u>two stressed syllables</u>, for example "Long, <u>long</u> shall I <u>rue</u> thee". The emphasis on these two syllables adds <u>weight</u> to his feelings of <u>regret</u>.

3) Lines <u>5</u> and <u>7</u> each have <u>three stressed syllables</u> — this <u>disrupts</u> the regular rhythm, hinting at a <u>loss of control</u>. The stressed words "<u>Pale</u>", "<u>cheek</u>" and "<u>cold</u>" in line 5 suggest the narrator's <u>anguish</u> at his lover's coldness and the <u>death</u> of their relationship.

The Farmer's Bride (Pages 12-13)

1) <u>Uneven line lengths</u> and the <u>lack</u> of a regular <u>rhyme scheme</u> create a <u>natural rhythm</u> that sounds like <u>speech</u>.

2) <u>Rhyming couplets</u>, <u>triplets</u> and <u>quatrains</u> increase the <u>pace</u> of the poem — this makes it feel as though it is <u>rushing</u> towards an <u>inevitable conclusion</u>.

3) In the final stanza, Mew uses <u>monosyllabic</u> words (e.g. "<u>Oh! my God!</u>"), <u>repetition</u> (e.g. "<u>her hair, her hair!</u>") and <u>caesurae</u> (e.g. "<u>The brown of her — her eyes</u>") to <u>break down</u> the rhythm. This draws attention to the farmer's loss of <u>self-control</u>.

Their eyes, their eyes — their tiny, tiny legs! I like sausage dogs, OK.

Rhyme schemes are important in other poems...

OTHER POEMS

Both 'Follower' and 'Love's Philosophy' use half-rhymes to show how something has fallen short of what the narrator desires. The regular ABACA rhyme scheme in 'Walking Away' reflects the steadiness of parental love.

Voice

The voice is a key feature of a poem — it can have a big effect on how the poet's message is conveyed.

1) Some poems are addressed to a specific person.
2) Poetry can reproduce spoken language to hint at the speaker's character.

Direct address can give clues about the nature of a relationship

When We Two Parted (Pages 2-3)

1) The narrator addresses his former lover directly, suggesting that he wants her to be aware of his pain — this highlights his bitterness, but it also shows that she's still important to him. The repetition of "thy" (your) and "thee" (you) emphasises his fixation with her.

2) The narrator uses "we" when talking about the past, and "I" and "thee" when talking about the present. This emphasises the distance between the narrator and his former lover.

Mother, Any Distance (Pages 22-23)

1) The narrator addresses his mother directly — this emphasises how important she is to him. No-one else is mentioned in the poem, which shows that their bond is unique.

2) The first word of each stanza emphasises his journey towards independence. The first stanza begins with "Mother", the second with "You" and the last with "I". This progression from "Mother" to "I" shows how he's moving from dependence to self-reliance.

Some poems include elements of spoken language

The Farmer's Bride (Pages 12-13)

1) Mew uses dialect words (e.g. "abed") and non-standard grammar (e.g. "she runned away") to create an authentic voice for the farmer and to draw the reader into the story.

2) His language helps to give him a recognisable identity as an ordinary farmer — this highlights the contrast between him and his quiet, animal-like, almost otherworldly wife.

Before You Were Mine (Pages 24-25)

1) The narrator addresses her mother directly, using colloquial language such as "your pals". This creates a conversational tone, which emphasises the closeness between the narrator and her mother.

2) Questions such as "whose small bites on your neck, sweetheart?" suggest that the narrator wants to engage in dialogue with her younger mother, but the lack of an answer emphasises that she can't.

Singh Song! (Pages 28-29)

1) Phonetic spellings (e.g. "vid" instead of 'with' and "di" instead of 'the') reflect the speaker's Indian accent — this shows that his Indian heritage is an important part of his identity.

2) The narrator uses both Indian words (e.g. "chapatti") and English words (e.g. "pinnie"). This shows that his identity is being formed by the merging of these two cultures.

Other poems use direct address...

The narrators of 'Sonnet 29' and 'Love's Philosophy' both make direct appeals to their lovers. 'Winter Swans' uses the voices of both the narrator and his lover, which gives an added insight into their relationship.

Beginnings of Poems

Poets know that first impressions are important, so there's usually something to say about openings of poems.

> 1) The <u>beginning</u> of a poem often <u>sets the tone</u> for the rest of the poem.
> 2) Poets aim to <u>draw in</u> their readers, and to establish something of the poem's <u>meaning</u>.

Some beginnings set the scene...

Structure is the way that poets order and develop their ideas in a poem. The beginnings and endings of poems are key structural devices.

Neutral Tones (Pages 10-11)

1) The <u>setting</u> of the "<u>pond</u>" on a "<u>winter day</u>" is established immediately. This creates a powerful image of a <u>cold</u>, <u>desolate</u> scene.

2) The narrator and his lover "<u>stood</u>" by the pond — their <u>inactivity</u> helps to establish the <u>lifeless</u> atmosphere that characterises the poem.

3) The words in line 1 are <u>simple</u> and mostly <u>monosyllabic</u>. This creates a <u>deadening</u> effect, which hints at the narrator's <u>grief</u> and sets up the '<u>neutral</u>' tone of the poem.

"We frolicked by a pond that summer day..."

Walking Away (Pages 14-15)

1) The first line establishes that "<u>eighteen years</u>" have passed since the events of the poem. The <u>caesura</u> before "almost to the day" highlights the fact that the narrator can still remember the <u>exact day</u>, which shows how <u>important</u> the memory is to him.

2) The detailed descriptions in the first stanza of the "<u>touch-lines new-ruled</u>" and the "<u>leaves just turning</u>" create a <u>vivid</u> picture of the scene, and also introduce the idea of <u>change</u> and <u>new beginnings</u>.

Eden Rock (Pages 18-19)

1) The opening introduces the <u>subject</u> of the poem — the narrator's <u>parents</u>. The fact that they are "<u>waiting</u>" for him hints at the <u>strong bond</u> between the parents and their son.

2) The narrator describes his father's "<u>same</u>" suit and the dog which is "<u>Still</u> two years old" — this makes it clear that the poem is based on a memory or a vision of the <u>past</u>.

3) <u>Vague language</u>, such as "<u>somewhere beyond</u>", hints at an element of <u>unreality</u>. The <u>heavenly- sounding</u> location of "<u>Eden Rock</u>" suggests that the setting could be an imagined <u>afterlife</u>.

...while others launch straight into the action

Climbing My Grandfather (Pages 30-31)

1) The poem begins with the narrator's <u>decision</u> to climb his grandfather "free" — the <u>verb</u> "<u>decide</u>" and the <u>end-stop</u> create a sense of <u>purpose</u> and <u>determination</u>.

2) The narrator's decision to climb "<u>without a rope or net</u>" introduces an element of <u>danger</u>, which grabs the reader's <u>attention</u>.

3) The use of the <u>present tense</u> makes the reader feel <u>close</u> to the action.

OTHER POEMS

You could write about the beginning of any poem...

The beginning of 'Before You Were Mine' introduces the idea of freedom and fun before motherhood. The opening lines of 'Porphyria's Lover' establish a gloomy mood and hint at the narrator's madness.

Endings of Poems

Relief might be your emotion when you reach the end of a poem, but please don't write that in your exam...

> 1) Poems often end with a <u>memorable</u> image or idea.
> 2) They can also end with a <u>twist</u>, which <u>changes</u> the reader's <u>understanding</u> of the poem.

Endings can sum up a poem

Mother, Any Distance (Pages 22-23)

1) The ending sums up the narrator's feelings about gaining <u>independence</u>. There are <u>dangers</u> — he might "<u>fall</u>" — but the "<u>endless sky</u>" offers <u>exciting opportunities</u> if he manages to "<u>fly</u>".

2) The <u>rhyme</u> of "<u>sky</u>" and "<u>fly</u>" and <u>alliteration</u> of "<u>f</u>all or <u>f</u>ly" emphasises the final two lines. This highlights the <u>central message</u> of the poem — the narrator's need for <u>independence</u>.

3) The <u>short last line</u> makes the couplet feel <u>unbalanced</u> and <u>incomplete</u> — this highlights that he <u>doesn't know</u> what will happen or whether he'll <u>cope</u>.

Winter Swans (Pages 26-27)

1) <u>Ending</u> the poem with a <u>couplet</u> emphasises how the narrator and his lover have come back <u>together</u>.

2) The simile comparing their hands to a "<u>pair of wings</u>" hints that the couple are <u>two halves</u> of a <u>whole</u>.

3) Their hands are like wings "<u>settling after flight</u>" — this <u>links</u> them explicitly to the swans who "<u>mate for life</u>", which hints that their relationship is <u>permanent</u>.

Endings can be surprising

Porphyria's Lover (Pages 6-7)

1) Line 58, "<u>And thus we sit together now</u>", is <u>shocking</u> — we realise that the narrator has been <u>sitting with</u> his murdered lover for the entire poem. The <u>sudden shift</u> from the <u>past</u> to <u>present tense</u> increases the <u>impact</u> of the revelation.

2) The final line is <u>ambiguous</u> — the narrator could be <u>triumphant</u> that he has <u>escaped</u> punishment, or he could be suggesting that the lack of punishment proves that he <u>hasn't</u> done anything <u>wrong</u>.

3) Victorian readers may have <u>expected</u> the narrator to be <u>punished</u> for his sin — the fact that he isn't could hint that Browning is <u>questioning</u> the <u>existence</u> of God.

Follower (Pages 20-21)

1) The sudden <u>role reversal</u> in the final stanza comes as a <u>surprise</u> — previously, the narrator "<u>stumbled</u>" behind his father, but now it is the father who is "<u>stumbling / Behind</u>". This suggests that he is no longer a <u>powerful</u>, <u>awe-inspiring</u> figure.

2) The <u>caesura</u> in line 22, the shift to the <u>present tense</u> and the <u>plosive</u> sounds in "<u>B</u>ut <u>t</u>oday" add <u>force</u> to the statement, which increases the <u>shock</u> of the reversal.

3) The narrator's statement that his father "<u>will not go away</u>" could suggest that his feelings of admiration and awe have been replaced with <u>irritation</u>.

Other poems feature interesting endings...

The final line of 'Eden Rock' is ambiguous — it isn't clear what the "it" the narrator refers to actually is. At the end of 'The Farmer's Bride', the reader is left to wonder what will happen to the farmer and his wife.

Mood

"Well, confused and desperate initially, but then I got this great revision guide. Oh, the mood of the <u>poem</u>..."

> 1) The mood is the <u>feeling</u> or <u>atmosphere</u> of a poem.
> 2) Poets use a <u>variety</u> of <u>techniques</u> to create mood.

The mood can stay the same throughout a poem...

Neutral Tones (Pages 10-11)

1) The poem has a <u>bleak</u>, <u>pessimistic</u> mood throughout. This is created by the <u>colourless</u>, <u>lifeless</u> setting and by the narrator's <u>attitude</u>.

2) The "<u>white</u>" sun and "<u>grey</u>" leaves convey a setting that lacks <u>warmth</u>, <u>joy</u> and <u>hope</u>.

3) The narrator believes that all "<u>love deceives</u>" and brings only <u>pain</u>, showing that his <u>faith in love</u> has been <u>damaged</u> by <u>bad experiences</u>.

4) The <u>slow pace</u> and frequent <u>repetition</u> of "<u>and</u>" create a <u>listless tone</u>, reflecting the narrator's <u>pessimism</u>.

Eden Rock (Pages 18-19)

1) <u>Enjambment</u>, <u>caesurae</u> and <u>half-rhymes</u> create a natural, gentle rhythm and a <u>peaceful</u> mood.

2) The <u>unhurried actions</u> of the narrator's parents contribute to this <u>tranquil</u> and <u>relaxed</u> atmosphere — his mother "<u>slowly</u>" prepares the picnic and they "<u>Leisurely</u>" beckon to him.

3) The peaceful mood suggests that the narrator finds the thought of meeting his parents again <u>reassuring</u>.

...or it can change

Winter Swans (Pages 26-27)

1) Initially, the poem has a <u>tense</u>, <u>unhappy</u> atmosphere. The couple are "<u>silent and apart</u>", which suggests that their relationship is <u>struggling</u>.

2) There is a gradual change of mood from <u>stanza three</u> onwards with the appearance of the swans. <u>Sibilant sounds</u> (e.g. "<u>s</u>low-<u>s</u>tepping") in the sixth stanza reflect the <u>easing</u> of the <u>tension</u>.

3) By the end of the poem, the mood is <u>peaceful</u> as the couple <u>reconnect</u> — the simile comparing their hands to "<u>a pair of wings settling after flight</u>" suggests <u>contentment</u> following <u>upheaval</u>.

Walking Away (Pages 14-15)

1) The mood in the first two stanzas is <u>anxious</u> — the images of a "<u>satellite / Wrenched from its orbit</u>" and a "<u>half-fledged thing</u>" suggest that the narrator thinks his son <u>isn't ready</u> to be independent.

2) The mood in the third and fourth stanzas is more <u>reflective</u>. The narrator uses the <u>gentle</u> image of a "<u>seed loosened from its parent stem</u>" to describe his son's first steps towards independence.

3) The final two lines have a <u>philosophical</u> tone — the narrator has come to the <u>understanding</u> that "<u>walking away</u>" and "<u>letting go</u>" are <u>necessary</u>.

'Porphyria's Lover' and 'Singh Song!' also have mood shifts...

In 'Porphyria's Lover', the narrator's sulkiness and passivity turn to contentment when he murders his lover. The quiet, intimate mood at the end of 'Singh Song!' contrasts with the noise of the shop during the day.

Practice Questions

It's the end of another section, so you know what that means — handy questions to see how well you've absorbed everything you've just read. Try to answer them without looking back through the section.

Forms of Poetry

1) Explain how 'Sonnet 29' differs from a traditional Petrarchan sonnet.

2) How does the form of 'Mother, Any Distance' reflect the narrator's love for his mother?

3) In 'Porphyria's Lover', how does Browning use form to show the instability of the narrator?

Poetic Devices

1) How does Shelley use repetition in 'Love's Philosophy' to emphasise the narrator's longing?

2) Give an example of repetition in 'Singh Song!' and explain its effect.

3) What is the effect of enjambment in 'Letters From Yorkshire'?

4) In 'Climbing My Grandfather', how does Waterhouse use caesurae to imitate the narrator's climb?

5) Give an example of an appeal to the senses in 'Before You Were Mine'. What effect does this have?

6) In 'When We Two Parted', how does Byron uses sensual imagery to convey the narrator's pain?

Use of Sound

1) How is onomatopoeia used in 'Before You Were Mine' to emphasise the impact that motherhood had on the narrator's mother?

2) Give an example of onomatopoeia in 'Sonnet 29' and explain its effect.

3) Choose an example of sibilance in 'Letters From Yorkshire' and describe the effect it has.

Imagery

1) How is the personification of nature in 'Winter Swans' used to comment on the couple's relationship?

2) In 'Love's Philosophy', how is personification used to strengthen the narrator's argument?

3) Find a metaphor or simile used to describe the narrator's father in 'Follower'. Explain what this shows about the narrator's feelings towards his father.

Practice Questions

Rhyme and Rhythm

1) Explain how Hardy uses rhyme in 'Neutral Tones' to emphasise the poem's message.

2) How does the rhythm of 'When We Two Parted' help to convey the narrator's feelings?

3) What is the effect of the breakdown of the rhythm in the final stanza of 'The Farmer's Bride'?

Voice

1) Why do you think Armitage chose to use direct address in 'Mother, Any Distance'?

2) What is the effect of the dialect words in 'The Farmer's Bride'?

3) In 'Singh Song!', how does the reproduction of spoken language reflect the speaker's identity?

Beginnings of Poems

1) How does the beginning of 'Walking Away' show the impact of the narrator's memory?

2) What does the opening of 'Eden Rock' tell us about the relationship between the narrator and his parents?

3) How does the opening of 'Climbing My Grandfather' draw the reader into the poem?

Endings of Poems

1) How is line 58 of 'Porphyria's Lover' shocking for the reader?

2) Explain how Heaney shows a change in the relationship at the end of 'Follower'.

3) Choose a poem not mentioned on page 57 and write about the effect of its ending.

Mood

1) What is the mood in 'Neutral Tones'? How is this mood created?

2) How does Causley create a peaceful mood in 'Eden Rock'? Why do you think he chose this mood?

3) Describe how the mood changes in 'Walking Away'. What does the change of mood suggest about the narrator's emotions?

Practice Questions

Here's your third and final batch of exam-style questions. Sections Four and Five have lots of handy advice about writing a great exam answer, so have a read of those pages if you're looking for some hints and tips.

Exam-style Questions

1) Compare the way that nature is portrayed in 'Love's Philosophy' and one other poem from 'Love and Relationships'.

2) Compare the presentation of fulfilment in romantic relationships in 'Sonnet 29 — I think of thee!' and one other poem from 'Love and Relationships'.

3) Compare the way that poets present memories in 'Before You Were Mine' and one other poem from 'Love and Relationships'.

4) Explore the ways in which distance is presented in 'Winter Swans' and one other poem from 'Love and Relationships'.

5) 'It may not always be easy, but it is crucial to appreciate your family.'

   Using this statement as a starting point, compare the appreciation for family in 'Climbing My Grandfather', and one other poem from 'Love and Relationships'.

   Remember to comment on how the poems are written.

The Poetry Exam

If you're doing AQA English Literature, you'll have to sit two exams —
this book will help you prepare for the Poetry Anthology section of Paper 2.

This is how your Paper 2 exam will work

1) The Paper 2 exam lasts for 2 hours and 15 minutes. It will be split into three sections, like this:

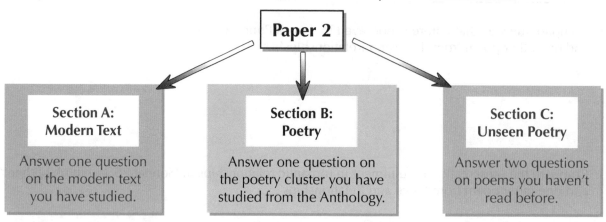

Paper 2

Section A:
Modern Text

Answer one question
on the modern text
you have studied.

Section B:
Poetry

Answer one question on
the poetry cluster you have
studied from the Anthology.

Section C:
Unseen Poetry

Answer two questions
on poems you haven't
read before.

2) The next few pages give you tips on how to answer the question in Section B.

3) Section B has one question about each poetry cluster. You should only answer one of these questions
— make sure you answer the question on the 'Love and Relationships' cluster.

4) Section B is worth 30 marks, which is about 20% of your entire GCSE. In the exam, you should spend
about 45 minutes on Section B.

5) You're not allowed to take your own anthology or any notes about the poems into the exam.

Read the question carefully and underline key words

1) Read the question for 'Love and Relationships' carefully. Underline the theme and any other key words.

2) The question will give you one poem and ask you to compare it with any other poem from the same
cluster. You'll be given a list of all the poems to help you choose — pick one that relates to the theme.

3) Here's the kind of question you'll get in the exam:

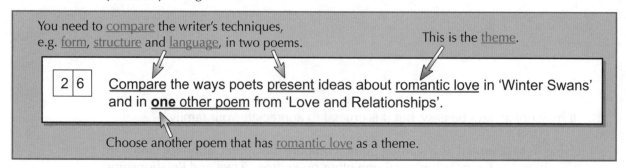

You need to compare the writer's techniques,
e.g. form, structure and language, in two poems.

This is the theme.

| 2 | 6 | Compare the ways poets present ideas about romantic love in 'Winter Swans' and in **one** other poem from 'Love and Relationships'.

Choose another poem that has romantic love as a theme.

There are three main ways to get marks

There are three main things to keep in mind when you're planning and writing your answer:

- Give your own thoughts and opinions on the poems and support them with quotes from the text.
- Explain the effects of features like form, structure and language.
- Describe the similarities and differences between poems and their contexts.

How to Structure Your Answer

A solid structure is essential — it lets the examiner follow your argument nice and easily. The best way to make sure you write a well-structured essay in the exam is to make a plan before you start writing (see p.67).

Start with an introduction and end with a conclusion

1) Your introduction should begin by giving a clear answer to the question in a sentence or two. Use the rest of the introduction to briefly develop this idea — try to include some of the main ideas from your plan.

2) The main body of your essay should be three to five paragraphs that compare the two poems.

3) Finish your essay with a conclusion — this should summarise your answer to the question. It's also your last chance to impress the examiner, so try to make your final sentence memorable.

Compare the poems throughout your essay

1) In each paragraph of the main body, write about one poem and then explain whether the other poem is similar or different. Don't just write several paragraphs about one poem, followed by several paragraphs about the other.

2) Every paragraph should compare a feature of the poems, such as their form, their structure, the language they use or the feelings they put across.

3) Link your ideas with words like 'similarly', 'likewise' or 'equally' when you're writing about a similarity. Or use phrases such as 'in contrast' and 'on the other hand' if you're explaining a difference.

Remember to start a new paragraph every time you start comparing a new feature of the poems.

Use P.E.E.D. to structure each paragraph

1) P.E.E.D. stands for: Point, Example, Explain, Develop.

> **POINT** — Begin each paragraph by making a comparison between the two poems.
>
> **EXAMPLE** — Then give an example from one of the poems.
>
> **EXPLAIN** — Explain how the example supports your opening point.
>
> **DEVELOP** — Develop your point by writing about its effect on the reader, how it links to another part of the poem, how it relates to the poem's context, or by adding to the comparison with the other poem.

After you've explained your first example, give an example from the other poem and explain that too.

2) This is just a framework to make sure your paragraphs have all the features they need to pick up marks — you don't have to follow it rigidly in every paragraph.

3) Here's an example of how you could use P.E.E.D. to structure a paragraph:

Start with a point that compares the two poems.

Give examples from both poems.

Explain how the examples relate to your opening point.

You can develop your point separately for each poem, or for both poems at the same time.

> Both 'Sonnet 29' and 'Singh Song!' use repetition to emphasise the narrators' joy in their relationships. In 'Sonnet 29', the word "thee" is repeated several times, which shows that the narrator's lover is never far from her thoughts. This is emphasised in the final line, where the double use of "thee" highlights the sense of bliss that she experiences when she is with him. Similarly, the final four stanzas of 'Singh Song!' repeat the phrases "I say", "she say" and "baby", which highlights the closeness between the narrator and his wife. This repetition creates a sincere tone, which contrasts with the humorous tone elsewhere in the poem, stressing the depth of their love.

Section Four — Exam Advice

How to Answer the Question

The exam is no time to discover your inner politician — you actually need to answer the question you're given.

Look closely at language, form and structure

1) To get top marks, you need to pay close attention to the techniques the poets use.

2) Analyse the form and structure of the poems, which includes their rhyme scheme and rhythm.

3) Explore language — think about why the poets have used certain words and language techniques.

4) You also need to comment on the effect that these techniques have on the reader. The examiner wants to hear what you think of a poem and how it makes you feel.

5) This is the kind of thing you could write about language:

> In 'The Farmer's Bride', Mew uses hunting imagery to portray the differences between her characters. She describes the bride using similes such as "like a hare" and "Shy as a leveret", which liken her to helpless prey animals and emphasise her vulnerability. Conversely, the husband states "We chased her" and "We caught her", casting him in the role of predator. This contrast creates a sense of uneasiness, which is heightened in the final stanza, when the narrator's use of exclamation marks ("Oh! my God!") and repetition ("her eyes, her hair, her hair!") suggest that he is losing control, and won't be able to curb his predatory instincts for much longer. In contrast...

Analyse the effects of key quotes.

Always develop your ideas.

Always support your ideas with details from the text

1) To get top marks, you need to back up your ideas with quotes from or references to the text.

2) Choose your quotes carefully — they have to be relevant to the point you're making.

3) Don't quote large chunks of text — instead, use short quotes and embed them in your sentences.

> ✘ Sheers compares the couple to the swans they see — "I noticed our hands, that had, somehow, / swum the distance between us / and folded, one over the other, / like a pair of wings settling after flight."

This quote is too long and it doesn't fit into the sentence structure.

> ✓ In 'Winter Swans', Sheers creates a link between the couple and the swans by describing the way their hands "swum the distance" and joined together "like a pair of wings".

These quotes are nicely embedded into the sentence.

4) Don't forget to explain your quotes — you need to use them as evidence to support your argument.

> ✘ The narrator in 'Climbing My Grandfather' learns about his grandfather. On his climb, he discovers "an earth-stained hand", "the glassy ridge of a scar", "the old stitches" and "a smiling mouth".

This just describes what happens in the poem.

> ✓ Waterhouse uses a physical voyage of discovery as a metaphor for learning the history of a loved one. The "glassy ridge of a scar" shows that the grandfather has experienced difficult, painful events, which have left their mark on him.

This explains how the quote supports the argument.

How to Answer the Question

The examiner doesn't have a list of right and wrong answers for this exam — you'll get plenty of marks for original or creative interpretations of the poems, as long as they're relevant and your points are developed well.

Give alternative interpretations

1) You need to show you're aware that poems can be <u>interpreted</u> in <u>more than one</u> way.

2) If a poem is a bit <u>ambiguous</u>, or you think that a particular line or phrase could have several <u>different meanings</u>, then <u>say so</u>.

> By the end of the poem, the narrator of 'Follower' seems frustrated that his father "will not go away"; the fact that he is "stumbling / Behind" suggests that, as an adult, the narrator feels hindered by his father's presence. However, the definite, matter-of-fact tone of "will not go away" could also hint at the close, unbreakable bond between father and son, and the son's unspoken understanding that his father will always be an important part of his life.

Remember to support your interpretations with evidence from the poem.

3) Be <u>original</u> with your ideas — just make sure you can back them up with an <u>example</u> from the text.

Show some wider knowledge

1) To get a top grade, you need to <u>explain</u> how the <u>ideas</u> in the poems relate to their <u>context</u>.

2) When you're thinking about a particular poem, consider these aspects of <u>context</u>:

Historical — Do the ideas in the poem relate to the <u>time</u> in which it's <u>written</u> or <u>set</u>?

Geographical — How is the poem shaped and influenced by the <u>place</u> in which it's set?

Social — Is the poet <u>criticising</u> or <u>praising</u> the <u>society</u> or <u>community</u> they're writing about?

Cultural — Does the poet draw on a particular aspect of their <u>background</u> or <u>culture</u>?

Literary — Was the poet influenced by other <u>works of literature</u> or a particular <u>literary movement</u>?

3) Here are a couple of <u>examples</u> of how you might use <u>context</u> in your <u>answer</u>:

> By referring to the "horse-plough", Heaney links his father to an earlier time, before mechanised farm equipment was common. The physical, skilled nature of this work emphasises the father's strength and expertise, but the reference also hints that his ability may not be relevant in the modern world.

> Porphyria acts in a way that would have been seen as sinful in Victorian times: she goes to visit a man on her own and flaunts her sexuality, for example by making her "white shoulder bare". In this way, the poem may have been read by contemporary audiences as a cautionary tale, in which a young woman is punished for her sins. However, the fact that the narrator remains unpunished for the far greater sin of murder prevents a simple interpretation of the poem.

How to Answer the Question

It's not just what you write that gets you a top grade — it's how you write it. Your writing style should be clear and precise, and you need to use the correct terms to show the examiner you know what you're talking about.

Use sophisticated language

1) Your writing has to sound <u>sophisticated</u> and <u>precise</u>.

> ✗ The narrator of 'Letters From Yorkshire' says lots of good things about living in the country.
>
> ✓ The narrator of 'Letters From Yorkshire' presents an idealised view of rural life.

Not very sophisticated.

This sounds much better.

2) It should be <u>concise</u> and <u>accurate</u>, with no <u>vague words</u> or <u>waffle</u>.

> ✗ Byron uses lots of words about death to emphasise the narrator's grief.
>
> ✓ Byron uses a wide range of references to death to emphasise the narrator's grief.

This is too vague.

Use more specific language.

3) Your writing should also show an <u>impressive range</u> of <u>vocabulary</u>.

Don't keep using the same word to describe something.

Vary how you say things — it sounds much more impressive.

> ✗ In 'Neutral Tones', the narrator feels bitter that his relationship ended. Describing his lover's smile as "the deadest thing" shows he feels bitter that she stopped loving him. His bitterness is also evident in his claim that "love deceives", showing that he can no longer trust lovers.
>
> ✓ In 'Neutral Tones', the narrator feels bitter that his relationship ended. Describing his lover's smile as "the deadest thing" emphasises his grief that she stopped loving him. His sense of loss is also evident in his claim that "love deceives", showing that he can no longer trust lovers.

4) However, make sure you <u>only</u> use words that you know the <u>meaning</u> of. For example, don't say that a poem has a '<u>volta</u>' if you don't know what it <u>really means</u> — it will be <u>obvious</u> to the examiner.

Use technical terms where possible

1) To get top marks, you need to use the <u>correct technical terms</u> when you're writing about poetry.

2) There's a handy <u>glossary</u> at the back of this book that <u>explains</u> these terms.

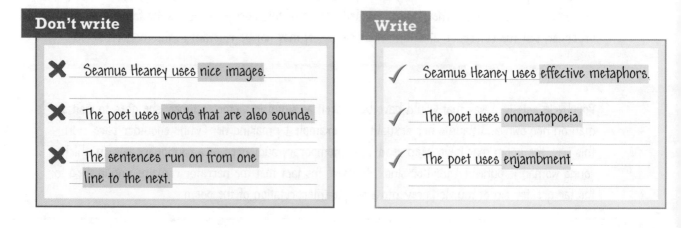

Don't write	Write
✗ Seamus Heaney uses nice images.	✓ Seamus Heaney uses effective metaphors.
✗ The poet uses words that are also sounds.	✓ The poet uses onomatopoeia.
✗ The sentences run on from one line to the next.	✓ The poet uses enjambment.

© Not to be photocopied

Planning Your Answer

In an exam, it's always tempting to launch straight into writing your answer, but this can end in disaster. Making a plan is the key to a sophisticated, well-structured essay. Trust me — it's worth it.

In the exam, spend five minutes planning your answer

1) Always <u>plan</u> your answer <u>before</u> you start writing — that way, you're less likely to forget something <u>important</u>.

2) Write your plan at the <u>top of your answer booklet</u> and draw a <u>neat line</u> through it when you've finished.

3) <u>Don't</u> spend <u>too long</u> on your plan. It's only <u>rough work</u>, so you don't need to write in full sentences. Here are a few <u>examples</u> of different ways you can plan your answer:

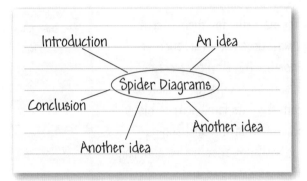

Bullet points with...
- Intro...
- An idea...
- The next idea...

Tables with...

A point...	Quote to back this up...
Another point...	Quote...
A different point...	Quote...

4) A good plan will help you <u>organise</u> your ideas — and write a good, <u>well-structured</u> essay.

Here's a sample question and plan

> **2 6** Compare the ways poets present the relationship between a parent and child in 'Walking Away' and in **one** other poem from 'Love and Relationships'. **[30 marks]**

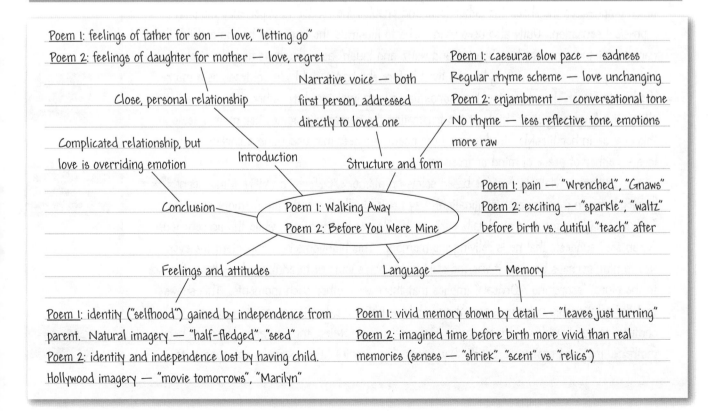

Sample Answer

Here's how you could use the plan on page 67 to write a really good answer.

'Walking Away' and 'Before You Were Mine' offer contrasting views of the relationship between a parent and a child. While 'Walking Away' is written from the perspective of a father watching his son's first steps towards independence, 'Before You Were Mine' focuses on a daughter's ironic regret that she didn't know her mother as a young woman, before her life was changed by having a child. Both poets explore the deep, loving bond between a parent and child, but also show that the relationship isn't straightforward or painless.

Refer to the question and the poems you're writing about in your opening sentence.

Sum up how the poems relate to the theme.

Both poets use form to help convey the feelings of the narrator for their parent, and the strong bond between a parent and child. 'Walking Away' uses caesurae, such as "That hesitant figure, eddying away", to slow the pace of the poem. The slow pace creates a sorrowful mood that mirrors the narrator's regret that his son is growing up, as well as reflecting the son's uncertain movement as he drifts away from the safe familiarity of his father's presence. However, the regular ABACA rhyme scheme hints at the unchanging nature of the love between the two, suggesting that "letting go" will not alter the relationship as much as the narrator seems to fear. Like Day Lewis, Duffy uses caesurae and enjambment, for example "I knew you would dance / like that." This creates a conversational tone, which highlights the intimacy between the narrator and her mother. In contrast to 'Walking Away', Duffy uses no rhyme. This gives the poem a more immediate, less reflective feel than 'Walking Away', hinting that the narrator's feelings of guilt and regret at bringing an end to her mother's "glamorous" life are still raw. This suggests that, although the narrator is close to her mother, their relationship is complicated.

Make sure you mention form and structure.

Explain how each point relates to the question.

Remember to develop each point.

Comment on similarities and differences between the poems.

Both poems use language to convey the negative aspects of parent-child relationships. In 'Walking Away', the father's anguish as his son leaves him is stressed by emotive verbs such as "Wrenched" and "Gnaws". Both of these verbs fall at the start of enjambed lines, which emphasises the shock the father feels and enables the reader to experience his pain as a physical sensation. Duffy also uses vivid verbs to illustrate the impact of having a child; the narrator pictures her mother "sparkle and waltz and laugh" as a young woman, the lively verbs mirroring the carefree, exciting life she lived before she had a child. In contrast, as a mother she has to "teach" her daughter, the monosyllabic verb implying duty rather than fun, whilst the alliterative "stamping stars" hints at the frustration the narrator imagines her mother feels at this change in her lifestyle. In this way, both poems suggest that becoming a parent involves loss — either of peace of mind or freedom.

Use the correct technical terms.

Integrate examples into your sentences.

Whereas 'Walking Away' is based solely on memory, 'Before You Were Mine' spans the border between memory and imagination. Day Lewis vividly recreates the memory of his son "walking away" by focusing on details such as the "leaves just turning", while the present tense "I can see" suggests that he is reliving the memory. This highlights how important the event was to him, perhaps because it was the start of his son's journey to adulthood — the reference to the plural "scorching / Ordeals" implies that there were other such moments. This shows that the relationship between a parent and a child is not static, but is constantly evolving. In contrast to Day Lewis's vivid memory, in 'Before You Were Mine' the narrator describes her mother's imagined past more vividly than her real memories. For example, she appeals to

Keep making comparisons between the poems.

Give a personal response.

Sample Answer

different senses by referring to her mother's "shriek", "scent" and the "small bites" on her neck, suggesting that she has built up a richly detailed picture of her mother as a young woman. Conversely, the narrator's memory of the empty "relics" of her mother's "high-heeled red shoes" suggests that the mother she knew was no longer a "glamorous" young woman; the shoes were just a reminder of her former self. This hints at the vivacious personality that the mother lost, and explains why the daughter longs for a relationship with the mother of her imagination.

Both poems focus on identity, but from different perspectives. Day Lewis suggests that a child's personality is shaped by independence from its parents. He uses a metaphor to compare the child to a "half-fledged" bird and a simile to liken him to a "winged seed". This links him to the natural world and suggests that the experience of "letting go" is something that every parent must go through in order for their child to develop. In contrast, Duffy explores the restrictions that parenthood brings and the effect of these restrictions on identity. Hollywood imagery, such as "movie tomorrows", hints at the mother's "glamorous" identity before she had a child. The reference to "Marilyn" (Monroe), a movie star whose life became turbulent and unhappy, hints at her mother's exciting early life and suggests that her later life was difficult. The description of her as a "ghost" could support the interpretation that her early identity was lost through parenthood, or alternatively it could hint that the mother has recently died, explaining the narrator's tone of regret and her preoccupation with thoughts and memories of her mother. In both poems, it is clear that the relationship between parent and child isn't just about love — it is also about sacrifice.

Both poems portray the relationship between parents and children as close and loving, but complicated. The parents in both poems make sacrifices for their children, and suffer because of this. While 'Walking Away' examines a father's painful decision to allow his relationship with his son to change, 'Before You Were Mine' explores the impact that a parent-child relationship has on a mother's life and identity. Despite these differences, the enduring impression from both poems is of deep attachment and love, showing that the parent-child relationship is one of the strongest bonds in nature.

Comment on the language the poets use, and the effect it has.

Bring in wider knowledge where you can.

Suggest more than one interpretation of the poem.

Explain how each point relates to the question.

Your last sentence should sum up your argument, and it needs to be memorable.

How to write a top grade answer

There's no single way of getting a grade 9, but these handy hints will help you on your way:

1) Be original — examiners get bored of reading the same thing over and over again, so coming up with your own interpretations will impress them (as long as you can back up your ideas with evidence).

2) Be critical — this means giving your own opinions about the poems. For example:

> The phrase "God-curst sun" compels the reader to experience the scene as Hardy's narrator does: a bleak, lifeless landscape, devoid of hope and forsaken by God.

3) Get to grips with context. It's not enough just to mention a link to context — you need to really explore the effect it has on the poem, or on your understanding of it. For example:

> The death of Causley's father when he was just seven supports the reading of the scene as an imagined afterlife, adding pathos to the narrator's vision of a reunion with his parents.

Section Four — Exam Advice

Adding Quotes and Developing Points

The next couple of pages will give you a chance to practise your P.E.E.D. skills by adding quotes and developing the points in some sample answers. Enjoy...

You can find the answers for this section on p.80.

Complete this plan by adding quotes and developing points

1) Below is an exam question and a plan for answering it.
2) Find quotes from the poems to back up each of the language points in the table (marked **A**, **B**, **C** and **D**).
3) Make brief notes on your personal response to each poem (marked **E** and **F**) to complete the plan.

> **0 1**   Compare the ways in which family relationships are presented in 'Eden Rock' and in **one** other poem from 'Love and Relationships'.   **[30 marks]**

	Eden Rock	Climbing My Grandfather
Themes and ideas	Strong parent-child bond, defies changes caused by time/death.	Physical and emotional exploration of Grandfather.
Language	Detailed memory ... **(A)** Language about light ... **(B)**	Mountain metaphors ... **(C)** Language of discovery ... **(D)**
Form and Structure	Regular form, half-rhymes, gentle rhythm. Separate final line.	Present tense, progress up mountain. Enjambment, caesura.
Personal Response	**(E)**	**(F)**

Add quotes to improve these answers

In the sample answers below, replace each letter (**A**, **B** and **C**) with a suitable quote.

> **0 2**   Compare how poets present feelings of longing in 'Love's Philosophy' and in **one** other poem from 'Love and Relationships'.   **[30 marks]**

Answer Extract 1

'Love's Philosophy' and 'Sonnet 29' both use natural imagery to emphasise feelings of longing. In 'Love's Philosophy', Shelley personifies nature, for example **(A)**, to suggest that all of nature craves intimacy. This adds weight to the narrator's argument that he and his lover should be together. Similarly, Barrett Browning's narrator compares her thoughts to **(B)** to show that her longing for her lover is uncontrollable. The natural metaphor extends to her lover, who she likens to a **(C)** about which she grows. This suggests that she yearns for his support.

Answer Extract 2

The narrator of 'Love's Philosophy' uses rhetorical questions, such as **(A)**, to make his lover question her refusal to be with him. This gives the poem a pleading tone, which emphasises the narrator's powerlessness in the face of rejection and helps the reader to empathise with him. In contrast, Barrett Browning uses imperatives such as **(B)** to try to hasten her lover's return. She suggests that his presence will cause her thoughts to **(C)**, suggesting that she feels burdened by her reflections when he is not there.

© Not to be photocopied

Adding Quotes and Developing Points

Have a go at developing these answers

1) Here are some more sample answers to question 2 on p.70.

2) In these extracts, the sentences followed by a letter (**A** or **B**) need to be developed further. Write an extra sentence to develop each point.

Remember — to develop your point you can write about its effect on the reader, how it links to another part of the poem, or how it relates to the poem's context.

> 0 2   Compare how poets present feelings of longing in 'Love's Philosophy' and in **one** other poem from 'Love and Relationships'.   **[30 marks]**

Answer Extract 1

'Love's Philosophy' has a regular ABAB rhyme scheme, reflecting the constancy of the narrator's feelings. However, half-rhymes such as "river" / "ever" create a note of discord, emphasising the narrator's sorrow at the fact that he and his lover are not together. **(A)**. 'Sonnet 29' also has a strong rhyme scheme, with half the lines ending with the same sound, for example "tree" / "see". This helps to drive the poem forward, reflecting the narrator's impatience to be reunited with her lover. **(B)**.

Answer Extract 2

Both 'Love's Philosophy' and 'Sonnet 29' use physical language to underscore the desire the narrators feel for their loved ones. Shelley repeats physical words associated with lovemaking, such as "kiss" and "clasp", to emphasise the relationship the narrator longs for. **(A)**. Conversely, Barrett Browning uses violent language such as "burst" and "shattered" to describe the effect the lover's presence has on the narrator's thoughts. Such words emphasise the intensity of her passion and the suddenness with which her thoughts are eliminated when her desire is fulfilled. **(B)**.

Answer Extract 3

Both poets use form to help convey a sense of longing. In 'Love's Philosophy', the final line of each stanza is shorter than the other lines, which makes it stand out. This adds weight to the rhetorical questions in each stanza, increasing the persuasive power of the narrator's argument. **(A)**. 'Sonnet 29' uses the sonnet form to link the narrator's feelings to a tradition of love poetry. However, the standard Petrarchan form is broken by the early arrival of the solution: "Rather instantly / Renew thy presence" appears in line 7, hinting that the narrator cannot wait for her lover's arrival. **(B)**.

   Section Five — Improving and Marking Sample Answers

Mark Scheme

Over the next few pages, you're going to put your examiner's hat on (I know, it's a dream come true) and mark some sample answers. This will help you to see what you need to do to get a great mark in your exam.

This section gets you to mark a range of sample answers

1) <u>Marking</u> sample exam answers is a <u>great way</u> to find out <u>exactly</u> what you need to do in the exam to get the grade you want.

2) Most of the answers in this section are only <u>extracts</u>, not <u>full answers</u>. The essay you'll write in the exam will be <u>longer</u> — more like the one on pages 75-76.

3) The mark scheme below is <u>similar</u> to the one that the <u>examiners will use</u> to mark your exam answers.

4) Read the mark scheme <u>thoroughly</u> and make sure that you <u>understand everything</u>.

5) Once you <u>understand</u> the mark scheme, use it to mark the sample exam answers on the next few pages. Don't forget to <u>explain</u> why you chose each grade.

Use this mark scheme to mark the sample answers

Grade band	What is written
8-9	• Shows an insightful and original comparison of the two poems • Effectively integrates a full range of precise examples to support interpretations • Closely analyses the poets' use of language, structure and form, making effective use of technical terms throughout • Gives a detailed exploration of how the poets' techniques affect the reader • Convincingly explores original and alternative interpretations of the ideas, themes, attitudes and context of the poems
6-7	• Presents a carefully thought out, developed comparison of the two poems • Integrates well-chosen examples to support interpretations • Explores the poets' use of language, structure and form, using correct technical terms • Examines the way the techniques used in the poems affect the reader • Gives careful consideration to the ideas, themes, attitudes and/or context of the poems, offering some original interpretations
4-5	• Gives a clear comparison of the two poems • Provides relevant detail to support interpretations of the poems • Explains how the poets have used some features of language, structure and form, using some relevant technical terms • Comments on how some of the techniques used in the poems affect the reader • Shows a clear understanding of the ideas, themes, attitudes and/or context of the poems

You can also be awarded <u>grades 1-3</u>. We <u>haven't included</u> any <u>sample answer extracts</u> at 1-3 level though — so those grades aren't in this mark scheme.

Marking Answer Extracts

Here's your first set of sample answers. For each one, think about where it fits in the mark scheme on page 72. Most answers won't fit the criteria for any one band exactly — it's about finding the best fit.

Have a go at marking these answer extracts

For each extract:

a)   Write down the grade band (4-5, 6-7 or 8-9) you think the answer falls into.

b)   Give at least two reasons why you chose that grade band.

> 0 3   Explore how a child's feelings for its parent are presented in 'Mother, Any Distance' and in **one** other poem from 'Love and Relationships'.   **[30 marks]**

Answer Extract 1

'Mother, Any Distance' and 'Follower' both use form to emphasise the narrators' feelings for their parents. 'Mother, Any Distance' has a loose sonnet form, which indicates the son's love for his mother. However, its rhyme scheme deviates from a traditional sonnet: the first stanza is loosely composed of rhyming couplets, and the number of end-rhymes generally decreases as the poem progresses. This reflects the son's efforts to move away from his mother's protection and become independent, though the close rhyme of "sky" and "fly" in the final two lines hints that their bond is unbreakable. 'Follower' is made up of six quatrains, with the regular, precise form reflecting each neat "furrow" of the ploughed field. This highlights the father's skill and the narrator's admiration for him. However, the regular form could also mirror the predictability of the father's life — this hints at the reason for the narrator's eventual decision not to follow in his father's footsteps, suggesting that a child's reverence for its parent may wane over time.

Answer Extract 2

Both poets suggest that a child's feelings towards its parents change over time. Armitage's narrator initially says that he "requires a second pair of hands", which shows that he needs his mother's help. But by the end of the poem he says "I reach / towards a hatch that opens on an endless sky", showing that he wants more independence from his mother. Likewise, in 'Follower', at first the narrator seems to worship his father, and wants to be like him — "I wanted to grow up and plough". In later years their roles are reversed, and he doesn't want to be like his father any more — "It is my father who keeps stumbling / Behind".

Answer Extract 3

Both poets use extended metaphors to show the narrators' feelings for their parents. In 'Follower', the father is described using nautical imagery, for instance his shoulders are like a "full sail strung". By illustrating the father's power, this simile highlights the son's awe of him. The narrator also compares his father to a ship's captain, who is capable of "Mapping the furrow exactly." This metaphor emphasises the father's skill. Like Heaney, Armitage uses an extended metaphor: the tape measure represents the bond between the narrator and his mother. The narrator's mother, "at the zero-end" of the tape, is compared to "base" and an "Anchor", showing that her son regards her as a permanent, stable presence in his life. This suggests that their relationship makes him feel safe and secure.

Marking Answer Extracts

You must be getting the hang of this now — if you get much more practice you'll be putting those English examiners out of a job. Remember to look out for comparison of the two poems in these extracts.

Have a go at marking these answer extracts

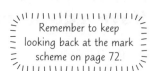
Remember to keep looking back at the mark scheme on page 72.

For each extract:

a)   Write down the grade band (4-5, 6-7 or 8-9) you think the answer falls into.

b)   Give at least two reasons why you chose that grade band.

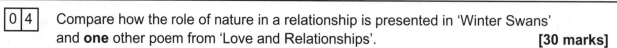

| 0 4 | Compare how the role of nature in a relationship is presented in 'Winter Swans' and **one** other poem from 'Love and Relationships'. **[30 marks]** |

Answer Extract 1

Both 'Winter Swans' and 'Letters From Yorkshire' present nature as a powerful force in a relationship. In 'Winter Swans', it is the observation that the swans "mate for life" that brings the couple together. This interjection of direct speech marks an end to the "silent" walk of the couple, and establishes a renewed emotional connection between them. This shows that the swans' actions have had a direct impact on the couple's relationship. Similarly, nature brings the narrator of 'Letters From Yorkshire' and the letter writer together. It is his wish to share the sight of "the first lapwings" with her that creates a connection between them. The alliteration and assonance in "word of that other world" draws out the phrase, which emphasises how important the letter writer's communications about the natural world are to the narrator. This shows that nature has helped to create a strong bond between them.

Answer Extract 2

In both poems, nature is linked to how the characters feel. In 'Winter Swans', nature reflects the couple's feelings. For example, the phrase "gulping for breath" suggests that their relationship is struggling. The word "gulping" sounds painful, like the couple have caused each other pain, or perhaps reflecting their tears. In 'Letters From Yorkshire', the characters' feelings seem to be affected by nature. For example, the man's "knuckles" are "singing" when he comes in from the cold, reflecting the way that nature has made him feel happy. The narrator seems to enjoy getting "word of that other world", showing how nature gives her pleasure too.

Answer Extract 3

Both poets use natural imagery to convey the distance between the couples. Sheers uses the swans to symbolise the couple: the swans "halved themselves" in the water, representing the emotional division between the couple, who walk "silent and apart". The metaphor likening the "halved" swans to "icebergs" creates an image of a cold, lifeless environment, which reflects the seeming demise of the relationship. Dooley uses natural imagery to highlight the distance between her protagonists' lives: the only way that the narrator can access the natural world that her correspondent inhabits is by him "pouring air and light into an envelope" for her. This active, natural metaphor contrasts with the narrator's static, artificial life of "feeding words onto a blank screen"; the image of her "feeding" the computer as if it were an animal underscores her desire to be more involved with the natural world.

© Not to be photocopied

Marking a Whole Answer

New page, new question and answer. Only this time it's the whole answer, not just an extract...

Now try marking this whole answer

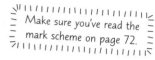
Make sure you've read the mark scheme on page 72.

a) Write down the grade band (4-5, 6-7 or 8-9) you think the answer falls into.

b) Give at least four reasons why you chose that grade band.

| 0 | 5 |

Compare how poets present the loss of love in 'Neutral Tones' and in **one** other poem from 'Power and Conflict'.

[30 marks]

'Neutral Tones' and 'When We Two Parted' both focus on the end of a relationship, and the feelings that this loss of love produces. Both poets use images of death to convey the grief experienced when love is lost, both address their former lovers directly to create a sense of personal loss and blame, and both imply that time brings no relief from these feelings. However, whilst for Hardy's narrator the main effect of lost love is sorrow and diminished faith in love, there are traces of anger and bitterness throughout Byron's poem, hinting perhaps that the loss of his lover damaged his ego as much as it did his heart.

Both poets use form and structure to emphasise the sorrow and pain of lost love. In 'Neutral Tones', the poem begins and ends with "a pond edged with greyish leaves". This circularity demonstrates that the narrator is unable to overcome his feelings of pessimism and hopelessness at the breakdown of his relationship. This is reinforced by the regular ABBA rhyme scheme — the repetition of the A rhyme at the start and end of each stanza hints that he cannot break free from the all-encompassing memory of his loss. The regular ABAB rhyme scheme of 'When We Two Parted' reflects the unchanging nature of the narrator's sorrow. Similarly, the repetition of "silence and tears" in the first and last stanzas shows how long-lasting his grief is, and suggests that he can picture no future release from it. Both poets also use a largely regular rhythm: in Hardy's poem this slows the pace and encourages the reader to identify with the narrator's feelings of depression, whereas in Byron's poem it propels the poem relentlessly onwards, hinting at the narrator's single-mindedness.

Hardy and Byron both use language associated with death to convey the sorrow experienced at the loss of love. For Hardy's narrator, the entire landscape is colourless, suggesting that nothing is living. The leaves are "grey" and even the sun, normally a symbol of warmth and life, is "white" and cold. This reflects both the death of his relationship and the desolation the narrator feels at the loss. Moreover, the "deadest thing" is the "smile" of his lover; this superlative hints that, while the rest of the world merely appears dead, their relationship stands no chance of resurrection. Similarly, by referring to his lover's "Pale", "cold" cheek, Byron's narrator likens her to a corpse, implying that the end of their relationship was similar to a death, over which he is still grieving. This effect is heightened by comparing the mention of her name to a funeral "knell": this monosyllabic word creates a deadening effect, and highlights the way that each new reference to the narrator's former lover brings him fresh grief.

Both narrators address their former lovers directly, which makes the poems seem more personal. In the first stanza of 'Neutral Tones', Hardy's narrator refers only to the collective "We"; in the second

---

This answer continues on page 76.

© **Not to be photocopied**   **Section Five — Improving and Marking Sample Answers**

Marking a Whole Answer

stanza he refers to he and his lover both as a couple ("us") and as individuals ("Your eyes on me"); and in the third and fourth stanzas he refers to them solely as individuals. This may reflect the gradual breakdown of their relationship, or the narrator's dawning realisation on "that winter day" that he had lost his lover. Similarly, Byron's narrator mostly uses the collective "we" to describe past events, and the singular "I" and "thee" to describe the present. This enhances the feeling of distance between the former lovers, emphasising the narrator's loneliness and regret. In both poems, direct address makes the reader feel that the women addressed and the events described are real, making the poems seem more intimate and heartfelt, and the sense of loss more poignant.

Sound is used in both poems to emphasise the pain and sorrow of loss, and the longevity of these feelings. Hardy uses alliteration in the phrase "wrings with wrong" to create a vivid sense of how the loss torments him. In addition, assonance of the long "oh" sound in words such as "rove", "Over" and "ago" in the second stanza lengthens the sound of the words, emphasising how "tedious" his former lover now finds him, and hinting that the loss of his lover has damaged his confidence and self-belief. Similarly, Byron repeats the long "ee" sound in words such as "thee", "grieve" and "deceive", with the lingering sounds reflecting the narrator's lasting sorrow at his lover's betrayal. Furthermore, his repetition of "sh" sounds in phrases such as "share in its shame" emphasises the "silence" in which he grieves for his loss. This confirms that he is unable to discuss his grief with his friends, which increases the reader's empathy for him.

The narrators of both poems hold others responsible for the pain they are enduring, perhaps hinting at the condemnation and bitterness that can stem from lost love. Hardy's narrator seems to blame his lover for the end of their relationship — his description of her "grin of bitterness" hints at his belief that she is taking pleasure in his pain. By referring to the "God-curst sun", he could even be suggesting that God is to blame for his suffering, or indicating that the loss he experienced has blighted his life to the extent that even the sun seems "curst". Byron's narrator refers to his former lover's "broken" "vows" and "shame", suggesting that he holds her responsible for the end of the relationship, and therefore for his suffering. The mention of "shame" and the emphasis on "silence" and secrecy adds weight to the theory that Byron wrote the poem for a married woman with whom he had an affair, who went on to conduct affairs with other men. If true, this could affect the reader's interpretation of the poem: rather than an outpouring of grief, the poem could be read as an expression of bitterness, with Byron mourning not lost love but rather wounded pride.

'Neutral Tones' and 'When We Two Parted' present vivid depictions of the long-lasting emotional anguish caused by the loss of love. Both compare the end of a relationship to a death, highlighting the grief that such a loss can cause, and both impart a sense of pessimism that their narrator will ever truly recover from the heartbreak experienced. However, whilst 'Neutral Tones' expresses heartfelt suffering at the breakdown of a relationship, there are hints that 'When We Two Parted' may be a reflection of Byron's irritation and resentment at being spurned, rather than the anguish of lost love.

Glossary

alliteration	Where words that are close together <u>start</u> with the <u>same sound</u>, e.g. "<u>wr</u>ings with <u>wr</u>ong".
ambiguity	Where a word or phrase has <u>two or more</u> possible <u>interpretations</u>.
assonance	When words share the same <u>vowel sound</u> but their consonants are different, e.g. "in this d<u>ee</u>p joy to s<u>ee</u> and hear th<u>ee</u>".
autobiographical	Describing something that happened in the <u>poet's life</u>.
caesura (plural <u>caesurae</u>)	A <u>pause</u> in a line of poetry. E.g. the full stop in "Over the drifted stream. My father spins".
chronological	When events are arranged in the <u>order</u> in which they <u>happened</u>.
colloquial	Sounding like everyday <u>spoken</u> language, e.g. "with your pals".
consonance	<u>Repetition</u> of a <u>consonant sound</u> in nearby words, e.g. "And fi<u>t</u> the brigh<u>t</u> s<u>t</u>eel-poin<u>t</u>ed sock".
dialect	A <u>variation</u> of a <u>language</u> spoken by people from a particular <u>place</u> or <u>background</u>. Dialects might include different words or sentence constructions, e.g. "When us was wed she turned afraid".
direct address	When the narrator of the poem <u>speaks directly</u> to another character, e.g. "long shall I rue <u>thee</u>".
dramatic monologue	A <u>form</u> of poetry that uses the assumed voice of a <u>single speaker</u> who is <u>not the poet</u> to address an <u>implied audience</u>, e.g. 'Porphyria's Lover'.
ellipsis	A series of dots which indicate a <u>pause</u>. It can add to a poem's <u>meaning</u>, e.g. in 'Mother, Any Distance', an ellipsis suggests how the tape measure is being stretched out.
emotive	Something that makes you <u>feel</u> a particular <u>emotion</u>.
empathy	When someone <u>understands</u> what someone else is experiencing and how they <u>feel</u> about it.
end-stopping	Finishing a line of poetry with the <u>end</u> of a <u>phrase or sentence</u>.
enjambment	When a sentence or phrase runs over from <u>one line</u> or <u>stanza</u> to the <u>next</u>.
first person	When a poet writes about themselves or their group, using words like "<u>I</u>", "<u>my</u>", "<u>we</u>" and "<u>our</u>".
form	The <u>type</u> of poem, e.g. a sonnet or a ballad, and its <u>features</u>, like number of lines, rhyme and rhythm.
free verse	Poetry that <u>doesn't rhyme</u> and has <u>no regular rhythm</u> or <u>line length</u>.
half-rhymes	Words that have a <u>similar</u>, but not identical, <u>end sound</u>. E.g. "plough" and "follow".
hyperbole	The use of <u>exaggeration</u> to <u>emphasise</u> a point.
iambic pentameter	Poetry with a <u>metre</u> of <u>ten syllables</u> — five of them stressed, and five unstressed. The <u>stress</u> falls on <u>every second syllable</u>, e.g. "I <u>think</u> of <u>thee</u>! — my <u>thoughts</u> do <u>twine</u> and <u>bud</u>".
iambic tetrameter	Like iambic pentameter but with a metre of <u>eight</u> syllables — four stressed and four unstressed. E.g. "Three <u>Sum</u>mers <u>since</u> I <u>chose</u> a <u>maid</u>".
imagery	Language that creates a <u>picture in your mind</u>. It includes <u>metaphors</u>, <u>similes</u> and <u>personification</u>.
internal rhyme	When two or more words in the <u>same line</u> rhyme, e.g. "The soft young <u>down</u> of her; the <u>brown</u>".
irony	When <u>words</u> are used to <u>imply the opposite</u> of what they normally mean. It can also mean when there is a difference between <u>what people expect</u> and <u>what actually happens</u>.
juxtaposition	When a poet puts two ideas, events, characters or descriptions <u>close to each other</u> to encourage the reader to <u>contrast</u> them. E.g. Dooley juxtaposes different lifestyles in 'Letters From Yorkshire'.
language	The <u>choice of words</u> used. Different kinds of language have <u>different effects</u>.
layout	The way a piece of poetry is visually <u>presented</u> to the reader, e.g. line length, how the poem is broken up into different stanzas, whether lines create some kind of visual pattern.
metaphor	A way of describing something by saying that it <u>is something else</u>, e.g. "icebergs of white feather". An <u>extended metaphor</u> is a metaphor that is <u>carried on</u>, e.g. the ship metaphor in 'Follower'.

Glossary

metre	The arrangement of stressed and unstressed syllables to create rhythm in a line of poetry.
monologue	One person speaking alone for a long period of time.
monosyllable	Words with only one syllable, e.g. "I had not thought that it would be like this."
mood	The feel or atmosphere of a poem, e.g. humorous, peaceful, fearful.
narrative	Writing that tells a story, e.g. 'Winter Swans'.
narrator	The person speaking the words. E.g. the narrator of 'Singh Song!' is a newly married shopkeeper.
onomatopoeia	A word that sounds like the thing it's describing, e.g. "clicking" and "pluck" in 'Follower'.
oral poetry	Poetry that is intended to be spoken aloud, rather than read.
oxymoron	A phrase which appears to contradict itself, e.g. "warm ice".
pathetic fallacy	Giving human emotions to objects or aspects of nature, in order to create a certain mood. E.g. in 'Porphyria's Lover', the "sullen" wind creates a gloomy, threatening atmosphere.
personification	Describing a non-living thing as if it has human qualities and feelings, or behaves in a human way, e.g. "And the sunlight clasps the earth."
Petrarchan sonnet	A form of sonnet in which the first eight lines have a regular ABBA rhyme scheme and introduce a problem, while the final six lines have a different rhyme scheme and solve the problem.
phonetic spellings	When words are spelt as they sound rather than with their usual spelling, e.g. "di" instead of "the". It's often used to show that someone is speaking with a certain accent or dialect.
plosive	A short burst of sound made when you say a word containing the letters b, d, g, k, p or t.
rhetorical question	A question that doesn't need an answer, but is asked to make or emphasise a point.
rhyme scheme	A pattern of rhyming words in a poem. E.g. 'When We Two Parted' has an ABAB rhyme scheme — this means that the first and third lines in each stanza rhyme, and so do the second and fourth lines.
rhyming couplet	A pair of rhyming lines that are next to each other, e.g. lines 3 and 4 of 'Mother, Any Distance'.
rhythm	A pattern of sounds created by the arrangement of stressed and unstressed syllables.
sibilance	Repetition of 's' and 'sh' sounds, e.g. "slow-stepping in the lake's shingle and sand".
simile	A way of describing something by comparing it to something else, usually by using the words "like" or "as", e.g. "beasts in stall / Look round like children at her call."
sonnet	A form of poem with fourteen lines, that usually follows a clear rhyme scheme.
stanza	A group of lines in a poem.
structure	The order and arrangement of ideas and events in a poem, e.g. how it begins, develops and ends.
syllable	A single unit of sound within a word. E.g. "all" has one syllable, "always" has two.
symbolism	When an object stands for something else. E.g. the vines in 'Sonnet 29' symbolise the narrator's thoughts, and the swans in 'Winter Swans' symbolise the couple's relationship.
syntax	The arrangement of words in a sentence or phrase so that they make sense.
third person	When a poet writes about a character who isn't the speaker, using words like "he" or "she".
tone	The mood or feelings suggested by the way the narrator writes, e.g. bitter, reflective.
voice	The characteristics of the person narrating the poem. Poems are usually written either using the poet's voice, as if they're speaking to you directly, or the voice of a character.
volta	A turning point in a poem, when the argument or tone changes dramatically.

Glossary

Index

A

admiration 21, 25, 39, 42, 57, 73
alliteration 2, 8, 10, 16, 24, 41, 52, 57, 74, 76
ambiguity 6, 18, 20, 57, 65
anger 3, 52, 75
assonance 16, 20, 41, 52, 74, 76

B

'Before You Were Mine' 19, 21, 23-25, 37, 39, 42, 44, 51, 52, 55, 56, 67-69
bitterness 11, 55, 66, 75, 76

C

caesurae 6, 8, 15, 16, 18, 20, 24, 26, 51, 54, 56-58, 68
'Climbing My Grandfather' 9, 15, 21, 30, 31, 37, 38, 42, 49, 51, 53, 56, 64
colloquial language 25, 55
consonance 52
context 62, 63, 65, 69, 72
contrasts 16, 17, 24, 27-29, 50, 51, 55

D

death 2, 3, 6, 7, 11, 19, 37, 38, 43, 51, 66, 75
desire 13, 36, 41, 49, 71, 74
destructive love 36, 41
dialect 12, 13, 55
direct address 2, 4, 8, 22, 38, 55, 75, 76
direct speech 27, 37
distance 9, 13, 16, 17, 19, 27, 40, 45, 55, 74, 76
dramatic monologue 7, 13, 49

E

'Eden Rock' 7, 11, 15, 18, 19, 25, 31, 38, 43, 56-58
ellipsis 10, 22
end-stopping 51, 56
enjambment 2, 6, 7, 10, 14-18, 20, 22, 30, 31, 50, 58, 68
excitement 9, 23-25, 30, 31, 37, 51, 52, 57
extended metaphors 9, 23, 31, 42, 53, 73

F

family relationships 15, 19, 21, 23, 25, 29, 31, 38, 39
'Farmer's Bride, The' 5, 7, 11-13, 16, 36, 41, 43, 45, 49, 54, 55, 57, 64
'Follower' 17, 19-21, 25, 29, 31, 39, 41, 42, 45, 53, 54, 57, 65, 73

forms of poetry 49
frustration 4, 5, 12, 13, 20, 36, 45, 50, 52, 65, 68
fulfilment 9, 27, 29, 37

G

getting older 15, 21, 23, 31, 42
grief 56, 66, 75
guilt 42, 68

H

half-rhymes 4, 12, 19, 20, 22, 36, 39, 58, 71
hyperbole 4, 22

I

iambic tetrameter 13, 21
identity 21, 29, 55, 69
imagery 2, 4, 6, 10, 12-14, 20-22, 28, 30, 38, 39, 42, 44, 45, 51, 53, 74
independence 14, 23, 38, 42, 50, 55, 57, 58, 68, 69, 73
irony 25, 68

L

'Letters From Yorkshire' 16, 17, 19, 21, 27, 31, 39-41, 45, 49, 52, 66, 74
longing 5, 7, 9, 17, 36, 41, 70, 71
loss 3, 15, 37, 66, 75, 76
'Love's Philosophy' 4, 5, 13, 36, 41, 45, 50, 53-55, 70, 71

M

madness 6, 7, 49, 51
memory 3, 11, 14, 15, 18, 19, 25, 44, 54, 56, 68, 75
metaphors 2, 8, 14, 16, 18, 22, 26-28, 30, 31, 53, 64, 69, 70, 73, 74
monosyllabic words 4, 16, 18, 28, 30, 54, 56, 68, 75
mood 54, 58
'Mother, Any Distance' 15, 22, 23, 29, 38, 42, 49, 50, 52, 55, 57, 73

N

nature 4, 5, 8, 9, 11-17, 26, 27, 41, 45, 52, 53, 70, 74
'Neutral Tones' 3, 10, 11, 13, 37, 43-45, 53, 54, 56, 58, 66, 75
nostalgia 19, 25

O

onomatopoeia 20, 44, 52
oxymoron 10, 30, 43

P

pain 2, 3, 10, 11, 14, 15, 22, 42, 44, 52, 54, 55, 58, 68, 74-76
pathetic fallacy 6
peacefulness 19, 27, 37, 58
personification 4, 10, 26, 45, 53, 70
pessimism 11, 44, 58, 76
phonetic spellings 28, 29, 37, 55
playfulness 5, 28
plosive sounds 8, 9, 52, 57
'Porphyria's Lover' 5-7, 13, 36, 40, 41, 43, 49, 51, 52, 56-58, 65
possessiveness 6, 7, 25, 41, 42
punctuation 8, 9, 51

R

rebellion 25, 28, 39
regret 2, 3, 39, 41, 54, 68, 69, 76
religious references 5, 7, 10, 14, 18, 57
repetition 2, 4, 6, 10, 12, 14, 15, 20, 24, 28, 36, 39, 41, 50, 54, 55, 58, 63, 75, 76
rhetorical questions 2, 4, 5, 12, 16, 42, 50, 70, 71
rhyme and rhythm 54
rhyming couplets 12, 49, 54, 57, 73
rhyming triplets 12, 54
Romanticism 5

S

senses 3, 24, 39, 51, 69
sibilance 8, 12, 26, 52, 58
similes 6, 8, 12, 14, 20, 24, 26, 28, 37, 53, 57, 58, 73
'Singh Song!' 9, 27-29, 37, 39, 50, 55, 58, 63
sonnet 9, 23, 49, 71, 73
'Sonnet 29 — 'I think of thee!'' 7-9, 13, 17, 27, 29, 36, 37, 40, 41, 45, 49, 51-55, 63, 70
sound 52, 76
spoken language 55
symbolism 12, 18, 38, 39, 43-45, 74

V

voice 55
voltas 8, 51

W

'Walking Away' 3, 14, 15, 23, 37, 38, 40, 42, 44, 53, 54, 56, 58, 67-69
'When We Two Parted' 2, 3, 37, 40, 43, 44, 51, 52, 54, 55, 66, 75
'Winter Swans' 5, 9, 11, 26, 27, 37, 40, 43, 45, 49, 51, 53, 55, 57, 58, 64, 74

Answers

These are the answers to the exercises in Section Five. They're only suggestions, so don't worry if what you've written doesn't match exactly — there are lots of possible answers.

Page 70 — Adding Quotes and Developing Points

Sample Plan

(A) "an old H.P. Sauce bottle"

(B) "The sky whitens as if lit by three suns"

(C) "reaching for the summit"

(D) "I discover / the glassy ridge of a scar"

(E) Slow pace and gentle rhythm create feeling of tranquillity — reflects narrator's pleasure in the scene.

(F) Physical closeness as narrator explores his grandfather — strong sense of their close emotional bond.

Answer Extract 1

(A) "the mountains kiss high heaven"

(B) "wild vines"

(C) "strong tree"

Answer Extract 2

(A) "Why not I with thine?"

(B) "Renew"

(C) "Drop heavily down"

Page 71 — Adding Quotes and Developing Points

Answer Extract 1

(A) This half-rhyme also emphasises the words "for ever", which underscores the narrator's desire for an eternal connection with his loved one.

(B) The end-rhyme "thee" is repeated four times, which emphasises the narrator's obsession with her lover and longing for him to return.

Answer Extract 2

(A) By suggesting that powerful entities such as mountains and the sun "kiss" and "clasp", Shelley implies that even the mightiest beings rely on physical union, which strengthens his argument that he and his lover should be together.

(B) The plosive sounds create the impression that her thoughts are exploding, which conveys to the reader the sense that she is unable to contain her excitement.

Answer Extract 3

(A) The short lines also slow the pace of the poem — this creates a sense of wistfulness, which emphasises the narrator's yearning for his lover.

(B) The enjambment of these lines emphasises the words "instantly" and "Renew", which further underscores the narrator's eagerness to see her lover.

Page 73 — Marking Answer Extracts

Answer Extract 1

I would give this answer a grade 8-9 because it gives a detailed analysis of the poets' use of form, uses the correct technical vocabulary and suggests an original alternative explanation of an example.

Answer Extract 2

I think this answer would get a grade 4-5. It makes a point comparing the poems, and it supports the point with quotes from the poems. To get a higher grade, the points need to be explained and developed, and the quotes should be integrated into the text.

Answer Extract 3

I think this answer would get a grade 6-7 because it makes a good point comparing the poems and starts to explain the effect of language. To get a higher grade, the answer needs to be more fully developed.

Page 74 — Marking Answer Extracts

Answer Extract 1

I would give this extract a grade 6-7 because it makes a point, gives examples from the text and starts to analyse language. To get a higher grade, the point needs to be developed more, e.g. it could comment on the effect on the reader.

Answer Extract 2

I think this answer would get a grade 4-5. This is because it makes a point comparing the poems and backs it up with examples that are briefly explained. To get a higher grade it needs to offer more explanation of how the quotes support the point.

Answer Extract 3

I think this answer would get a grade 8-9 because it integrates examples from the poems, explains them effectively with plenty of technical terms, and develops the points made about them.

Pages 75-76 — Marking a Whole Answer

I think this answer should be awarded a grade 8-9 because it makes a wide range of detailed, original comparisons, focuses on the effects of form, structure and language on the reader and gives well-explained examples of the poets' techniques. It also refers to context and uses this to offer an alternative interpretation of one of the poems.